S0-AIB-030

Venetian Opera

IN THE

SEVENTEENTH CENTURY

Venetian Opera

IN THE
SEVENTEENTH CENTURY

BY

SIMON TOWNELEY WORSTHORNE

OXFORD

At the Clarendon Preß

Oxford University Press, Ely House, London W.1

GLASGOW NEW YORK TORONTO MELBOURNE WELLINGTON
CAPE TOWN SALISBURY IBADAN NAIROBI LUSAKA ADDIS ABABA
BOMBAY CALCUTTA MADRAS KARACHI LAHORE DACCA
KUALA LUMPUR SINGAPORE HONG KONG TOKYO

√ML
1703
.W 931
1968

FIRST PUBLISHED 1954
REPRINTED LITHOGRAPHICALLY IN GREAT BRITAIN
(WITH SUPPLEMENTARY BIBLIOGRAPHY)
AT THE UNIVERSITY PRESS, OXFORD
BY VIVIAN RIDLER
PRINTER TO THE UNIVERSITY
1968

Preface

One of the programmes for the Antient Concerts during 1845 includes a *scena* from Cesti's *Orontea*.[1] But in general the music of the seventeenth century has only lately attracted interest and, in consequence, given pleasure. The history of the opera both in this and the following century is however still little known. And the aim of this study has been to trace the origins of the component parts that were to make it an independent and new art form. The men who wrote the first works of this nature were as conscious as their successors in the nineteenth century that an opera cannot be enjoyed 'by reading a romance of Goethe in a picture-gallery adorned with statues, during the performance of a Beethoven symphony'. There is always the element of the *Gesamtkunstwerk* in its nature. And for this reason, in a general history of opera, it is difficult to do justice to the various factors that combine to make the successful work. It is only in a narrow field that the origins of the music, the poetry and the stagecraft can be traced before they fuse into the whole.

The Venetian *favole in musica* discussed in this book are the first works to be produced under more or less modern conditions, and have therefore a particular importance for the reader interested in the history of a form that played so vital a part in late seventeenth- and eighteenth-century life. For the opera, perhaps more than any other art, occupied the minds and satisfied the tastes of musicians and the general public at the time. To speak of the general public in connexion with opera before 1637 is perhaps an anachronism. For performance was then confined, for reasons of expense and social custom, to the numerous European courts. But the opening of the first public opera house in Venice meant that the performances could be financed from the sale of tickets. Venetian noblemen formed companies to build and speculate in opera houses, and the rows of boxes were rented by their friends or by travellers who flocked to the city to enjoy the new art. There is no question of distinguishing the kind of audience that attended these performances with the audience of an older generation. The importance of the opening of the public opera house lies rather in the permanent employment it gave to musicians. An opera was per-

[1] Theodore Martin, *The Life of His Royal Highness The Prince Consort*, London, 1875, vol. i, p. 497.

formed now for a season instead of once or twice during one series of special festivities at a court. A great number of people were able to see it, and the habit of going to the opera grew up in society. The opera became a part of the cultivated life which resulted in the birth of an informed and critical public, a phenomenon that has played so important a part in the development of music. A love of it quickly spread from Venice to Europe at large, so that an enthusiast could write of a famous singer of the part of Venus,

Io piutosto vorrei te sempre udire
Soavissima Venere canora
Ch'in grembo ad altra Venere gioire.

In a general history of the subject, it is difficult to discuss more than the music, for upon it will ultimately depend the life of a work. But the choice of a small yet prolific and formative period has enabled me to attempt a history not only of the music but of the librettos and stage design that have played an important part in the general development of the art. For in its early stages an opera was considered to have been written not by the composer but by the poet. And its success depended largely on the skill of the stage designer and engineer. Evelyn was more astonished by the changes of scenery at the opera in Venice than by the music. And the librettos were printed, when an engraved score was a great rarity. The composer's name usually remained unknown. But it did not take long for the public to appreciate the true balance.

The choice of Venice for this study does not depend entirely on its position as the first centre for opera. For companies sprang up quickly throughout Italy. But Venice for various reasons, from its unique position, its government by an oligarchy not averse to speculation, and the peculiar state of its political and economic situation in the seventeenth century, provides an interesting subject. It had a far greater number of opera houses than any other city in Europe; the *Contarini* collection of scores provides adequate material for a study of the music, and the *Marciana* library possesses one of the finest collections of librettos in Italy with a wealth of information in the prefaces that throws new light on methods of production, and the general attitude of producer and audience as it developed during the century. There is no study of the period available in English. Pioneers in the field were Hugo Goldschmidt, Henri Prunières, and Egon Wellesz whose books are still standard works on the subject. The studies on Monteverdi in the last few years have greatly increased our knowledge of operatic performances in the first half of the seventeenth century; but Hermann Wolff's scholarly book dealing with the opera in Venice during the second half of the century has been the only recent work on the period. However it has been found that the ramifications of these early productions have been so far reaching in their effect on music in general, and in creating the traditions that have governed opera itself both musically, and in its relation to the artistic needs of the societies in which it flourishes, that the present work, dealing with the growth of the music, poetry, and stage practice in Venice into its modern form, may serve as a complement to his work. For opera is a mirror of fashion. 'Vitae imitatio, Consuetudinis speculum, Comoedia.'

In writing the book I have been fortunate in having so many friends to whom I could turn for information and advice. My work was made easy by the interest and never failing help shown me in the *Marciana* library, by Professor Edward Ruffini the founder of the Luca Ruffini Scholarship, and by Count Giustiniani and numerous Venetians who made me free of their libraries, help for which I was most grateful. But above all I am obliged to Dr. Egon Wellesz who guided, informed and encouraged me at all times, and without whose support the book could never have been written.

I have to acknowledge my debt to the Director of the Bibliothèque de l'Opéra, Paris, to the Trustees of Sir John Soane's Museum, London for permission to reproduce drawings in their possession, to the Librarian of the Warburg Institute, London, for the loan of librettos, and to Dr. Frank Harrison and also to Mr. Dennis Rhodes of the British Museum for their help with the proofs.

S. T. W.

WORCESTER COLLEGE
OXFORD
October 1953

Contents

List of Plates

The proscenium arch has been cut from some of the plates of *Il Bellerofonte* and of the *Apparati Scenici* to allow greater space for the sets themselves

The Background to Opera in Venice

It is a curious if unwelcome fact that political liberty and intense artistic activity are not concomitant. Indeed, the arts would appear to flourish best under a government in which an authority is personified —an Augustan age, be it Burgundian or Medicean, regal, or seigniorial. The unwieldy despotism of the Spanish Habsburgs under Philip IV was also the great literary period of Spanish history; the Naples of Vico, the Scarlattis and Salvator Rosa was ruled by Spanish or Austrian governors; the Paris of Lully and Couperin, Molière and Racine bent to the will of Louis XIV. Yet, in this society, opera quickly assumed the conventions that govern it today. In fact it is largely the product of political circumstances and has itself played a large part in the moulding of events. The uses to which opera has been put in the politics of Europe would make a fascinating study, which would run like a thread from its origins until almost the present day. The Italian troupe engaged by Mazarin in 1648 became a political weapon with which to abuse the cardinal on the broadsheets of Paris:

> . . . icy venir de si loin,
> A force d'argent et de soin,
> De ridicules personnages
> Avec de lascives images . . .[1]

The story of the rival styles of French and Italian opera involving Louis XVI and Marie Antoinette is well known; Verdi became a figure-head of the *risorgimento*, and the Empress Eugenie turned her back on the stage because of the opinions expressed in *Don Carlos*; Auber's *La Muette de Portici* gave the signal for the revolt which established Belgian independence; these are only a few instances of the powerful part opera has taken as a means of political expression. And even in its origins we can see the influence of events. For it was not entirely fortuitous that Venice became the first great centre for opera on a large and intensive scale, the effect of which has not found a parallel until the coming of the cinema.

---

[1] Henry Prunières, *L'Opéra italien en France avant Lulli*, Paris, 1913, p. 148.

B

By 1637, the date of the opening of the first opera house in Venice, the State had shown herself to be independent of both Rome and of the great secular powers. And of all the Italian States she alone had withstood the papal claims of ecclesiastical jurisdiction; in spite of the interdict of 1606, she had emerged triumphant after the struggle associated with the name of Paolo Sarpi. In the dispute over the Mantuan succession, Venice ranged herself on the side of the Duke of Nevers, a Gonzaga but of French upbringing, and was thus an ally of Henry IV and Urban VIII until the conclusion of a settlement in 1631. It is true that success in Europe was partially offset by a war against the Turks in the Aegean. But such a threat was indirectly the means of binding to herself allies against an enemy who might threaten, not Venice alone, but Europe and the Christian world. In fact, we find that, whereas in 1623 the Legate, Cardinal Agucchi, complained of the caesaro-papalism of Venice and of her friendship with the Turk,[1] in 1638 Urban VIII allowed Venice to raise a tenth from all ecclesiastical benefices for the prosecution of a war.[2] In practice the war hardly worried the people as a whole, and in no way affected the popularity of Venice as what may be called the tourist centre of Europe. This connexion with the Mohammedan world, as we shall see later, was artistically useful, since it made Venice the 'clearing house' for all the bizarre habits and clothes brought by trade and war, and stimulated the imagination of her artists.

In this connexion, too, the researches of scholars played a part. The great antiquarian and secretary to the literary Accademia patronized by Cardinal Barberini, Giovanni Battista Doni, advised producers to dress their players according to the nation and century they desired to portray.[3] And the new interest taken in post-classical antiquity would be of assistance in this aim. The Accademia della Crusca, founded for the compilation of an Italian dictionary in 1582; the spoliation of classical Rome by the Barberini to provide material for the great baroque buildings; the excavations under St. Peter's to find the tomb of the saint—all indicate a new facet of antiquarian research.

As a city Venice presented much the same appearance as it does today. The *Dogana* and the church of Santa Maria della Salute were as

---

[1] Ludwig von Pastor, *History of the Popes*, London, 1939, vol. xxix, pp. 176–7.
[2] Ibid., vol. xxviii, p. 362.
[3] Giovanni Battista Doni, *Lyra Barberini*, Florence, 1763, ed. A. F. Gori, vol. ii, p. 9.

yet unbuilt. But for the most part the city's geography has remained unchanged.[1] It was governed by a hierarchy[2] that gave most of the nobility some office or privilege to ensure allegiance. Inclination kept them in the city. But, in addition, by complicated and far-reaching laws, the small oligarchy of real rulers bound the nobility to dependence on the State, by means of a policy akin to that used later by Louis XIV in France. The rich, not encouraged to mix with foreign visitors or diplomats, turned the banks of the Brenta into delicious gardens in perspective topped by Palladio's elegant villas, some of them with their own theatres; one of the most remarkable of these was Marco Contarini's at Piazzola near Padua where sumptuous spectacles were given.[3]

It is to Marco Contarini largely that we owe our knowledge of the opera of the period, from the collection of one hundred and twelve scores known as the *Codices Contariniani* in the Marciana Library, Venice, left to the State by one of his descendants. And the communal life of a highly organized state concentrated within the confines of a small city kept alive interest in such diversions as opera. A performance was talked of, every phrase savoured, the merits of singers canvassed and individual performances remembered as a matter of course. And the pleasure it gave was increased by an intimate knowledge of previous performances.[4]

The audience for these spectacles was drawn from the whole community rather than from one class, although it was financed by the rich Venetian aristocrats. There is, however, no justification for attributing the peculiarities of opera in Venice to the peculiar form of society found there. If the new art form is not always intellectual, it cannot be said to derive from any popular expression of artistic taste dependent upon a 'democratic' government, since Venice was as much encased in the niceties of social distinction as any other seventeenth-century society.[5] But a long tradition of public entertainment had made every citizen a connoisseur of spectacle. And it is interesting to note

[1] See map from Vincenzo Coronelli, *Viaggi del P. Coronelli*, Venice, 1697, vol. i, p. 43. (Given as plate 1.)

[2] Pompeo Molmenti, *La storia di Venezia nella vita privata*, Bergamo, 1908, pt. 3, vol. i, ch. i.

[3] Taddeo Wiel, *I Codici Musicali Contariniani*, Venice, 1888, p. viii.

[4] Pompeo Molmenti, op. cit., ch. vi, and *Venezia alla metà del secolo XVII*, Relazione inedita di Mgr. Francesco Pannocchieschi, Rome, 1916.

[5] Pompeo Molmenti, 'Venezia nel Sec. XVII descritta da due contemporanei' in *Emporium*, vol. xlviii, no. 288, Venice, 1918.

how intelligent a Venetian audience seems to have been in the early
days of opera, for, although it was a popular entertainment, it was
popular as Greek drama was popular. It is significant that the overtures were written in what is now called the French style of grave–
allegro–grave and the prologue declaimed by a single voice in recitative. The audience had not to be hushed by a flurry of trumpets as
had been the case at courtly festivities and was to become so again in
Naples. And, when Venice became the international drawing-room of
Europe, during the last quarter of the century, we find composers falling into line with the taste of an audience more interested in themselves than the stage. Fanfares and loud overtures, however, had been
used from the very first in the princely courts as a means of quietening
the fashionable throng, as we can see from the score of Monteverdi's
Orfeo. Saint-Didier, the French traveller, remarks on the fashionable
concourse at a time when the fame of the opera was drawing crowds
to the city. 'Voilà', he writes, 'en quoy Venise fait consister l'essence
de sa liberté; mais rien ne rend la sujection plus douce au peuple, que
de voir qu'il n'y a point de plaisir à Venise, qui ne luy soient communs
avec la noblesse.'[1] Economically this social habit resulted in the popularity of the public opera house and enabled the impresario to produce
on a lavish scale from his box-office takings. The free and easy atmosphere made it the goal of all who liked to enjoy themselves. Saint-
Didier continues: 'La fameuse liberté de Venise y attire les étrangers
en foule, les divertissemens, et les plaisirs les y arrêtent, et épuisent
leur bourse: les grands Seigneurs, et les Princes Souverains y vont souvent pour quelques temps; l'usage commode de *l'incognito* joint aux
charmes de la liberté Venitienne, leur font sacrifier de grandes sommes
à leur plaisirs.'[2] Carnival time was the height of the season when, under
cover of the mask, all liberties were allowed; but, besides this season,
lasting from 26 December to Shrove Tuesday, there were two
shorter periods from the Ascension until 15 June and from 1 September
to 30 November when the playhouses were open.

Of the two great musical centres of the time, Rome and Venice, the
latter offered greater scope for the dramatic composer. Rome, under
Urban VIII, had been very much entertained by his nephews the
Cardinals Barberini with the new art. But there was a difference in

[1] Alexandre de Saint-Didier, *La Ville et la République de Venise*, Paris, 1680, p. 355.
[2] Ibid., p. 395.   [3] Henry Prunières, *Cavalli*, Paris, 1931, p. 17.

PLATE I

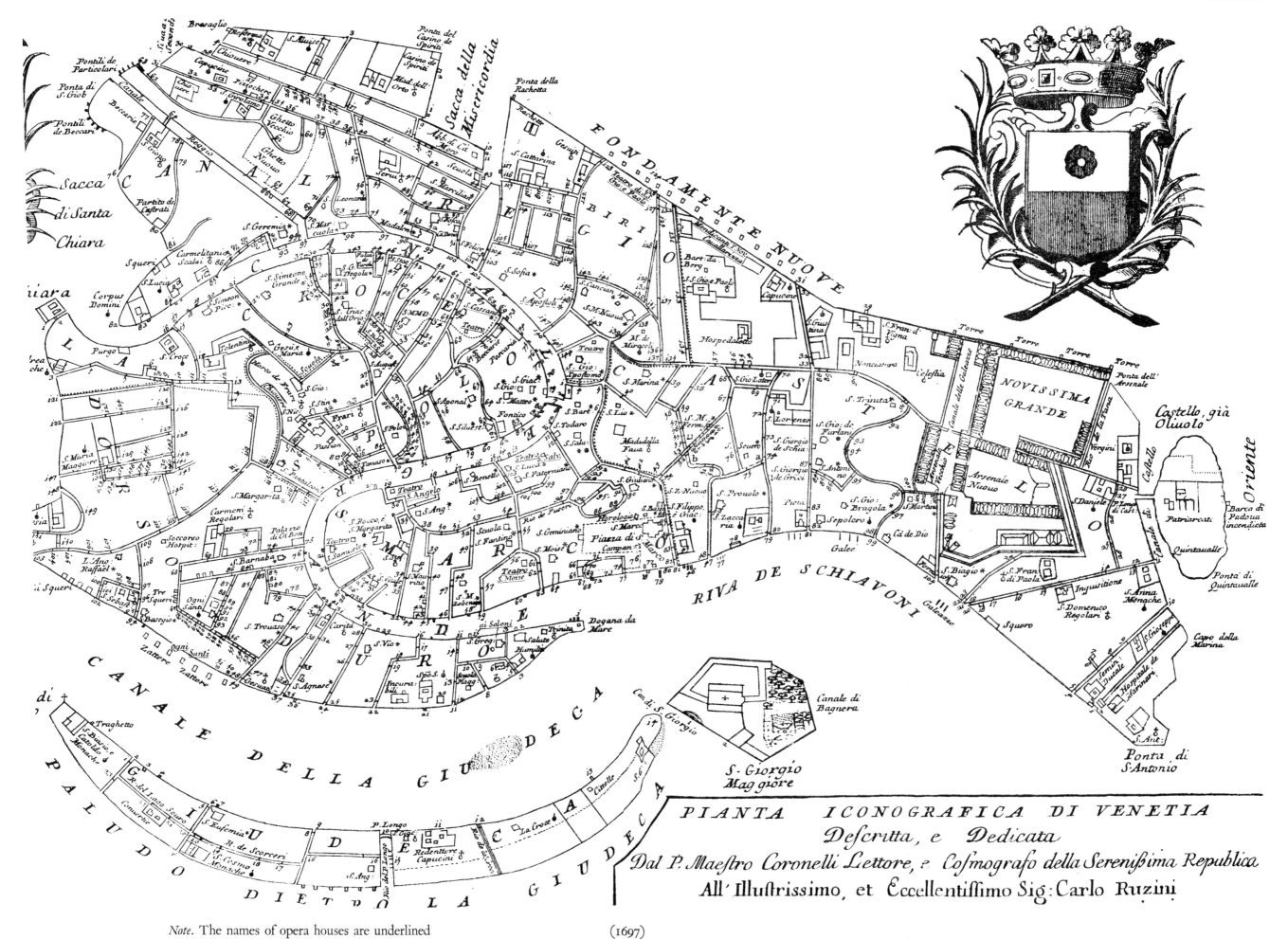

PIANTA ICONOGRAFICA DI VENETIA
Defcritta, e Dedicata
Dal P. Maeftro Coronelli Lettore, e Cofmografo della Serenißima Republica
All' Illuftrissimo, et Eccellentißimo Sig: Carlo Ruzini

Note. The names of opera houses are underlined   (1697)

outlook between the two cities. The early operas in the Palazzo Barberini were given before a large audience of distinguished and cosmopolitan people as part of an entertainment lasting for some hours. Each undertaking depended upon the enthusiasm and riches of some patron, and, naturally the choice was dictated largely by the whim of the Pope himself.

The Barberini fortunes, however, were partly responsible for the shift of the operatic centre away from Rome. On 10 May 1637 Urban VIII was taken seriously ill at Castel Gandolfo. He returned to Rome in June still dangerously ill, and only entirely recovered in August. Meanwhile the city had become a barracks filled with troops of the various princely Italian cardinals. The Barberini nephews themselves commanded a body of Corsican mercenaries. Conditions in Rome at the time have been described as bearing 'a striking resemblance to the wildest periods of the Middle Ages'.[1] These conditions may have helped to keep the Manelli–Ferrari company in Venice. For this partnership, the earliest operatic touring company, must have moved there about February 1637 in order to prepare *Andromeda*. It may have found that the freedom of running its own theatre, and the immediate success of the new public entertainment, offered greater promise of further triumph than the return to dependence upon the patronage of an insecure if powerful family, who, for the moment, could ill afford the time for new entertainments. For, in spite of a calmer atmosphere in the following year, social life in Rome would always depend upon political considerations, and artists would be the servants of a prince. As it was, in March 1639, the last opera sponsored by the Barberinis, *Chi soffre, speri*, was staged. In November the Duke of Parma arrived in Rome to settle some territorial claims with the Pope. This visit led to the war of Castro which fully occupied the Barberinis and turned central Italy into a battlefield. It was ultimately the cause of their flight to France and the rupture with the Pamfili Pope Innocent X in 1645.

Since the theatre is essentially a social organization, successful performances require secure conditions in which to flourish. Rome, under the Popes, dependent upon individual tastes, was more conscious of the insecurity of patronage than other states, even in times of peace. It becomes clear that, in these years, crucial for the development of

---

[1] Ludwig von Pastor, op. cit., vol. xxix, p. 374.

the new musical form, it was essential for the artists to settle where they could exercise their own ingenuity, independent of the whims of magnates already overburdened by the direction of their own precarious fortunes. And Venice offered the necessary security to which no other Italian state could pretend, a security in which neither religion nor faction interfered with the even course of life. Such a precarious basis as that offered in Rome, firm enough to produce occasional brilliant performances, provided artists with opportunities different from the regular productions of Venice, which were dependent upon public taste and changed as inevitably as the weekly programme in the modern cinema. We find an observer[1] from Rome remarking on the general love of the theatre amongst all classes in Venice that shows at once its position in the social life of the Republic. 'The cost to anyone who wished to see a performance', he writes, 'was half a scudo [about three shillings], and almost anyone could afford it since money flowed in Venice.'[2] But amongst the many causes which established the taste for opera in Italy was the arrangement by which the theatres themselves were equipped with boxes; an auditorium was lined in fact with little rooms which became a part of the appurtenances of every well-to-do family. It is certainly necessary to seek for some such external cause to which we may attribute the sudden and intense interest in this fecund form of art. The idea of opera of course was certainly established long before 1637. Monteverdi's style is almost always dramatic. And, although there are extant no works of this nature between *Orfeo* of 1607 and the Venetian operas dating from 1641, as Shrade says, 'Monteverdi had never interrupted his dramatic work since he left Mantua' in 1612. 'The guiding principle that gave all his compositions a dramatic character can help the imagination to reconstruct the style of these lost dramas, and the few extant scenic compositions, including the ballo (dell'Ingrate), offer further assistance.'[3] The Venetian nobility were in no sense behind the rest of Italy in their appreciation of the new music drama. In fact, some of the earliest examples were performed before the Doge to entertain Henry III of France on his way to Paris to be crowned in 1574. The custom of giving annually these *favole*

---

[1] Pannocchieschi, Conte d'Elci, Secretary to his uncle, Mons. Scipione di Pannocchieschi, Papal Nuncio, Venice, 1647–52.

[2] 'La spesa che si ricerca a chi vuol vedere non passa in tutto che la metà di uno scudo, et quasi ognuno in Venetia, senza suo grande incommodo, lo può spendere, perchè il denaro vi abonda.'

[3] Leo Schrade, *Monteverdi*, New York, 1950, p. 345.

pastorale began in 1571, to celebrate the victory of Lepanto.[1] Einstein[2] considers them to differ from later operas only in that they are not so called. But it is unlikely that the whole play was set to music. In spite of the fact that accounts describe the performance in which 'tutti li recitanti hanno cantato in suavissimo concento, quando solo, quando accompagnato' a study of the casts will show that specific mention is made of musicians who sing or play the lute as distinct from the rest of the cast who presumably speak, at any rate, for part of the time. But we may judge these performances to be the immediate predecessors of the *dramma per musica*: the music must have resembled that written by Andrea Gabrieli for the chorus in *Oedipus Rex* with which the famous palladian Teatro Olimpico at Vicenza opened in 1585. Here a solo has short interjections in the choral singing.

But whatever success these early works may have had, and however anxious the Venetian nobility may have been to offer dramatic entertainment at home to their friends, we cannot find here the sole cause for the burst of enthusiasm which swept over Europe soon after the opening of the first public opera houses. It lies as much in the nature of opera itself, for 'wherever it has flourished', to quote Egon Wellesz, 'it has been accepted as an important factor in the nation's spiritual life. Every effort has been made to give it a permanent place among activities of the human spirit which are the justification of our civilization.'[3]

In its history opera quickly became more than an entertainment: although governments may have seen in it a harmless alternative to political agitation, it occupied the attention of the most active minds of the century and was used as a new and powerful means of emotional and intellectual stimulus. The various concepts which found expression in the symbols and images of seventeenth-century painting and literature could be made effective equally in a new way by means of the developing art. In this connexion Mario Praz penetrates the nature of opera in a passage from his book on Imagery: 'If considered from a philosophical angle', he says, 'the opera as a fusing together of various arts is purely an illusion; but from a psychological point of view it witnesses to a kind of imagination which tries to overreach itself, an

[1] Angelo Solerti, 'Le Rappresentazioni musicali di Venezia, 1571–1605', *R.M.I.*, 1902.
[2] Alfred Einstein, *The Italian Madrigal*, Princeton, 1949, p. 549.
[3] Egon Wellesz, *Essays on Opera*, London, 1950, p. 138.

appetite of the intellect as uncontrolled as an appetite of the senses; in a word, it argues a process of materialisation rather than of sublimation.'[1] It was not long before the old mythological plots, for example, gave way to subjects drawn from history only thinly disguised to provide the intrigues and interests of contemporary life; they were soon to be the vehicle of political expression, as indeed they have often remained. Wotquenne,[2] for example, lists a libretto in the Royal Library at Brussels, *La Lanterna di Diogene* (1674), in which each character represents a European sovereign, the key of which he found in a manuscript inside the printed copy.

The Venetian littérateur, Christoforo Ivanovich, had a shrewd idea of the cause of this sudden interest in the theatre when he mentions the lease of boxes as a useful and secure form of income for the owner or manager.[3] The Venetians had themselves formed companies in which the sale of the rights to boxes provided a substantial part of the funds. This method of leasing is still in existence in Italy today. The box itself is rented annually, but a fee allowing entrance into the theatre itself has to be paid for each performance. In the seventeenth century a certain number of free *biglietti d'ingresso* were allowed to members of an opera company as the theatrical papers in the State archives of Venice show.[4] The document here constitutes an

[1] Mario Praz, *Studies in 17th Century Imagery*, London, 1939, p. 12.

[2] Alfred Wotquenne, *Catalogue de la Bibliothèque du Conservatoire Royal de Musique de Bruxelles*, Annexe 1, Libretti d'opéras et d'oratorios italiens du XVIIᵉ siècle, Brussels, 1901, p. 90.

[3] Christoforo Ivanovich, *Minerva sulla Tavolina*, Venice, 1681, ch. x: 'e questa è stata la causa principale, che si siano fabricati più teatri con tanta facilità e prestezza.'

[4] Archivio de Stato, *Teatri*, Busta 914 (Documenti varii 1665 a dì 2 Luglio in Venezia): 'essendo che nel negᵒ di far recitar opere in Musica nel Teatro a San Salvatore il Sig. Gerᵐᵒ Barberi hà interesse di cinque sesti et è Prõne di cinque sesti di Habiti, Scene, e ogni altra sorte d'utili, et materiali di esso teatro, in riguardo che dell' altro sesto è Prõne l'Ecc S. Nicolò Minato: et ritrovandosi esso Sig. Gerᵐᵒ debitore del Sig: Marco Mozzoni di ducati cinquecento et venti dal 654 ducati per occasione di altrettanti esborsati per lui per servitio della recita dell' Opera del Carnovale prossᵒ passato, nè avendo miglior modo da sodisfarlo, et così contentante il diᵒ Sig. Mozzoni, per ciò il Iᵒ Sig: Gerᵐᵒ li dà, cede rinontia, et assegna in pagamᵗᵒ due delli detti cinque sesti di Capitale, et interesse, che come sopra tiene in dᵒ teatro, li qti due sesti vengono a rilevar il 3ᵒ di tutto l'interesse, e Capitale sudᵒ, qte per consequenza esso Sig: Mozzoni per dᵃ portione doverà esser Prõne assoluto, potendone disponer à suo piacere dovendo subentrare per dᵃ parte in ogni luoco, stato ragione, et essere di dᵒ Sig: Gerᵐᵒ e far recitare ó concorrere à far recitare per dᵃ portione, come doverebbe fare esso Sig: Gerᵐᵒ et essendo anco obligato al pagᵗᵒ del' affito del teatro dᵃ portione: dovendo per l'incontro haver anco la 3ᵃ parte di tutto l'utile de' Palche, ed poca altra cosa proveniente da dᵒ Teatro, come si haverebbe esso Sig: Gerᵐᵒ così, che q̃sto per tal portione non habbi da ricevere più beneficio, ne risentire aggravio alcuno, ma tutto sia interesse del medᵐᵒ Sig. Mozzoni. Il qte stante la p̃nte cessione, e rinontia si chiama pago, et soddisfatto delli sudᵗⁱ Ducati 500 di suo credito, promettendo in essi nè in causa di essi mai più

agreement drawn up between three men of whom one is Count Nicolò Minato, a writer of many librettos and later court poet to the Austrian emperor. It illustrates both the direct interest in the management of affairs shown by the aristocracy and the security with which theatrical ventures were regarded, even to the extent of being accepted as bonds for a debt. The success of such ventures, from a financial point of view, encouraged the councils of provincial towns to adopt similar methods with the intention of improving the public amenities out of the profits.[1] These documents also emphasize the view of the box as a personal possession. The box was gained by ballot and the rent was owed to the city. But it is clear that any additional decorations the owner might require were his responsibility and should not be charged to the landlord's account. Gasparo Torelli, the restorer of the San Salvatore theatre,[2] has left accounts of his fees, in the Bergamo town council books, charged for the building of the municipal theatre. His charge was 'di far la scena del teatro, scene machine, palcho pitura delle sene [*sic*]' plus a charge for decorating 'il soffito proscenico et l'esteriore del Teatro'; the whole costing 7,882 Filippi. The manuscript includes the charges in full with details of the cost of the different materials and objects required. The *Mercure Galant* put the cost of a machine in San Salvatore in the opera *Le doe Tiranni*[3] (1679) as at 2,000 écus and adds the salaries of the chief singers. The castrato and leading female soprano received 400 pistoles for two months with the rest of the cast

pretendere, o dimandare cosa alcuna. Et all' incontro prometendo esso Sig: Ger^mmo di sollevare esso Sig. Mozzoni da qualcunque persona chi pretendesse attione contro d^a robba, così che egli non abbia da ricevere nel dominio di q^lla alcuna molestia. Riservandosi esso Sig: Ger^mmo per li doi pross^i Carnovali venturi, il suo Palco à pè Pian, et dovendo esso Sig: Mozzoni per la portione che à Lui s'aspetta concorrer con gli altri à concederli in tutto il Carnovale bolettini No. 27, da essergli dati à suo piacere per entrar all' opera senza pagarli, oltre li quali non possa pretendere l'ingresso nè della sua persona, nè d'altri per Lui, ma di qll^i debba essere contento, e sodisfatto. Essendo in oltre obligato esso Sig: Mozzoni à concorrere per sua parte à lasciar, che li Scagni siano posti in d^o Teatro da qll^o che è solito à ponerli; et ciò per li doi pross^i venturi Carnovali solam^te col pag^to però dovuto di qll^i. Et così promettono et si obligano le parti sud^te di mantenere, et osservare inviolabil^to sotto obligat^e in forma. In fede di che Io Gerolamo Barberi aff^mo et prometto q^do di sopra.'

[1] See documents for the City Council Books at Crema in Appendix 1.

[2] Preface to *Ariberto e Flavio*, 1685, performed 'in un teatro che deve la restauratione totale al Sig Gasparo Torelli'.

[3] *Mercure Galant*, April 1679, p. 63: 'On n'avait pas esté quite de cette Machine pour deux mille Ecus. Joinez à cela les meilleurs Musiciens qu'on eust pû trouver. Le fameux Cortonne en estait. On leur donnait quatre cens Pistoles d'or pour deux mois de Représentation que dure le Carneval; autant à Marguerite Pia, deux cens cinquante à la Signora Giuglia Romana, et aux autres selon leur mérite.'

on a sliding scale, whilst in *San Giovanni Grisostomo*[1] the three leading parts, including the famous Siface, the friend of Purcell, had a total salary of about 1,000 pistoles. The cost of Giacomo Torelli's *Orfeo* scene in Paris was 550,000 livres.[2] And the Journal of Dubisson-Aubernay[3] for 2 January 1648 states: 'Le sieur Corneille avait recu deux mille quatre cents livres et le sieur Torelli, gouverneur de Machines de la pièce d'Orphée, ajustandes à celle-ci plus de douze mille livres.' This new interest in music as a means of increasing trade is remarked in his diary by an eye-witness in the early days:

And in the plays or, as they say, works in music, they give them in Venice in every ample and exquisite form, competing to make them more respected. Besides, they are the industry of the people, the wealth of the country itself whence it seems they have had their origins and where equally it will suffice to say they perform them more as business than pleasure.[4]

But it was the box which had an influence that permeated through the whole organization and captured the public on other grounds than consideration of business. It became simply another room in a rambling mansion, the obvious means of cramming as many people as possible into a confined space, yet preserving the amenities of a civilized social life. For, if St. Mark's Square can be considered today as the drawing-room of Europe, the box was then the boudoir from which the world of politics and fashion could be discussed and plans for future policies laid. 'Presque tous les nobles', says a French satirist of the following century, 'ont leur maison au théatre, qu'ils appellent, où ils habitent, mangent, jouent et boivent: du moins y ai-je vu des gens y dormir tres-profondément.'[5] The feeling of ownership was enhanced for the hereditary principles were implicit in the lease. The box belonged to

---

[1] Ibid., p. 66: 'Neron estait le titre de l'Opéra qui fut representé sur ce Théatre. Le fameux Isape ou Josepin de Bavières, l'incomparable Jean François Grotti [*sic*] Romain, surnommé Siphax, et la Signora Antonia Caratti Romaine, y chantoient. Ces trois avoient pour eux seuls mille Pistolles d'or pour leur Carneval.'

[2] S. Wilma Holsboer, '*L'Histoire de la mise en scène dans le théâtre français de 1600 à 1657*, Paris, 1933, p. 237.   [3] Ibid., p. 237.

[4] Pompeo Molmenti, *Venezia alla metà del secolo XVII*, Relazione inedita di Mons. Fr. Pannocchieschi, Roma, 1916. These documents are in the Archivio del Stato, Venice, and are the journal of the secretary to the Papal Nuncio Mons. Scipione de' Pannocchieschi, uncle to the author, who was in Venice from 1647 to 1652. 'Et quanto alli Teatri, overo come essi dicono le Opere in Musica, si rappresentano in Venetia in ogni più ampla et esquisita forma, concorrendo a renderli più riguardevoli, oltre l'industria della gente, l'opulenza del proprio Paese, d'onde pare che habbino tratto l'origine et ove parimente basterà di dire che le si fanno quasi più per negotio che per trattenimento.'

[5] Sara Goudar, *L'Espion chinois ou l'envoyé secret de la cour de Pekin*, Cologne, 1765, vol. ii, p. 143.

a family in the sense that so long as the rent was paid the contract could not be broken, and at the death of the tenant for life it passed, like entailed property, to the heir. Indeed the procedure as outlined by Ivanovich follows much the same lines as the English law of entail.[1] The security of tenure must account for the elegant decorations which were characteristic of the date. 'Ce n'est que de l'or au dehors des Loges le dedans tapissé de Velours de Dames, et des plus riches Etofes qui se fassent à Venise.'[2] But if these boxes were smartly decorated, they were at the same time snug, holding about three persons in front.[3] The plan of SS. Giovanni e Paolo shows a little withdrawing-room behind each box and closely resembles the scene at La Scala which caused Burney to remark that 'across the gallery of communication is a complete room to every box, with a fireplace in it, and all conveniences for refreshments and cards'.[4] And it was here perhaps that business, other than attending to the performance, was conducted. For example, the French ambassador assured a friend that it is necessary for all diplomats to attend the opera regularly because there it was possible to discover secrets which would be concealed from them in the ordinary course of events. 'Il ne faut pas croire que, quoique la noblesse vénitienne ne puisse avoir aucun commerce avec les ambassadeurs (sévérité bien sage), les ministres étrangers ne soient pas dans une sorte de liaison avec les magistrats; on se parle par des tiers; on se dit bien des choses par des signes à l'Opéra, circonstance qui rend la fréquentation des spectacles et les usages du masque nécessaires aux ministres étrangers.'[5] The English resident was once compelled to complain to the government that the box normally given to him by virtue of his position had been overlooked. The note adds:

[1] Christoforo Ivanovich, op. cit., ch. x: 'Si conviene in un affitto annuale, e si paga ogni volta, che in quell' anno fa recitar il teatro, non altrimenti venendo fatto questo pagamento in riguardo della spesa, che impiega il Teatro, e del comodo, che riceve chi lo tiene ad affitto. I "Ius" poi, che acquista il possessore d'esso Palchetto si è di tenerlo per sua propria ragione, senza facoltà di cederlo ad altri, di più d'adoprarlo per uso suo, e d'imprestarlo à beneplacito. Per due capi può ritornare al Padrone del Teatro, ò quando non viene pagato annualmente l'affitto sudetto, quando si recita, ò quando viene abbandonato volontariamente da chi lo possede; e in questi casi può passar à nuova locazione, altrimenti acquistato una volta sola si possede, durante la vita del Possessore, non meno che doppo la di lui morte, dagli Eredi, cioè dal Padre passa nel figlio, e dal figlio al Padre, e dal fratello al fratello, con la continuazione dell' obligo già convenuto dal principio, senza alcuna alterazione à quanto s'avesse praticato per il passato.'

[2] *Mercure Galant*, April 1679, p. 66.

[3] Ibid., March 1683, p. 230.

[4] Charles Burney, *The present state of Music in France and Italy*, London, 1773, p. 84.

[5] Pompeo Molmenti, *La storia di Venezia nella vita privata*, vol. iii, p. 408, n. 2.

'he did not care for music, esteem poetry or understand the stage, but merely desired it for the honour of his office, as his predecessor and all the other residents at present at the court enjoy the favour'.[1]

It is not particularly remarkable that the government should take adequate precautions to preserve public order in the many theatres that sprang up in Venice. But it is remarkable to find that the Doge himself allotted boxes to the heads of foreign missions. Yet such was the case; and the procedure laid down entered into every detail.[2] Pro-formas were issued by the government department concerned. Once the form was completed, the Doge drew lots for all the boxes in each theatre with the exception of the stage boxes, those already held by other diplomats, and that which belonged to the minister's immediate predecessor. If the box did not suit, a further draw could be made, but the proprietor of the original always lost his box. The owner of the box concerned in the second draw moved into that drawn originally. In this way there could be no hint of collusion between a Venetian and the minister.

It does not seem far-fetched, in the light of such evidence, to attribute the immediate interest shown in the new art to causes which, in some measure, lie beyond the purely musical and involve the economy of the city itself, the official prosecution of which demanded the interest and co-operation of the highest authority. The social convenience of the box encouraged an easy-going approach to the opera. The audience had no need to attend throughout each performance. But the amenities offered drew them to the theatre almost nightly, so that the scores were in the end thoroughly well known, the capabilities of individual singers assessed against the highest standards gained by experience,

[1] Calendar of State Papers, Venice, 1671–2, p. 152.
[2] Archivio del Stato, Busta 914 (Inquisitore di Stato, Ambasciatore stere [sic]): 'Metodo che si tiene dai Ministri per recercare li Palchi: Si presentano con Memoriale come dagli uniti Esemplari, all' Ecc^ma Consulta. Da questa col mezzo d'un Secretario de Senato viene ricercato il Serenissimo di far l'estrazione delli Palchi respettivi. Egli imbossolando tutti li Palchi di quell' Ordine ch'è relativo al carattere di quel Ministro che lo ricerca, fà l'estrazione di uno a sorte Si eccetriano li Procennii ed il Pargoletto li Palchi tenuti dagl' altri Ministri e quello ch'era tenuto dal Ministro ultimamente partito. Poi col metodo che s'indicherà qui avanti se ne avvanza l'avviso tanto al Ministro, che al Proprietario ed alla Consulta.

Quando il Palco estratto non accomoda a quel Ministro, egli avanza le sue ricerche alla Consulta perchè gli venga cambiato e con lo stesso metodo viene ricercato il Serenissimo d'una nuova estrazione. Egli in tal caso imbossolando solo i palchi in faccia liberi, fà una nuova estrazione e avvanza gli avvisi correspondenti, avvertendo il Proprietario del Secondo Palco, ch'egli avrà il godimento dell' altro Palco, che fu dapprima estratto.'

and an informed taste built up, which alone provides a fertile ground
for a flowering of the arts.

Still, apart from what may be called the sociological background to
the new art, it may seem inevitable to us that the style of musical
declamation with which composers were concerned from about 1600
should develop into opera, that is to say a dramatic performance with
rules and aims distinct from the ordinary stage. But the Florentine
school of Giovanni Bardi had no such aim in view. They wished to
revive Greek tragedy in its original, as they believed, trappings, declaiming their lines in a cantillation. 'Si doveva imitar col canto chi
parla',[1] Peri wrote. But they realized the limits to their knowledge of
ancient music and were not even certain that the recitative was his-
torically correct. They were only certain of its effectiveness. However,
they soon appreciated the dramatic qualities latent in the idea. Marco
da Gagliano gave detailed instructions in the preface to his *Dafne*
(1608) regarding the gestures of the singers, and excused himself
wisely saying, 'ho voluto scriver questa minuzia, perchè è più impor-
tante ch'altri non pensa'.[2] And Monteverdi made his distinction
between the *prima pratica* or polyphonic style and the *seconda pratica*
or personally expressive style.

Realism was a characteristic of the Venetian school, inherited from
the earlier composers, and maintained by the intellectual attitude of
the day. But the difference between the sixteenth-century madrigalists
and the following century's monodists was clear cut. The former constantly employed vivid methods of portraying individual words but
for the latter, it was the mood of the whole piece that mattered. The
arts existed to move the soul by playing on the various moods or
affections, a conception capable of greater development than literal
transcription of words into music. It led in the end to the distinction
between the tone of different instruments and the peculiar effect each
had upon the hearer, a fact already noticed by the Greeks and re-
emphasized by the Jesuit father Menestrier in his book in which he
compares ancient with modern musical practice: 'Par ces changemens
de ton qui s'entrechoquent les uns les autres, et par le mélange de leurs
accords, souvent, comme nous voyons, ils causent à l'âme un transport,

---

[1] Angelo Solerti, *Gli albori del melodramma*, Milan, 1904, vol. ii, p. 109, from Peri's preface to
Euridice (1600).
[2] Angelo Solerti, op. cit., vol. ii, p. 72. Preface to Marco da Gagliano's *Dafne*.

et un ravissement admirable.'[1] But, although such a distinction was made in the latter part of the period under discussion in this work, it is an early example in the general history of music of an appreciation of tone colour. The aim of the earliest opera composers was less complicated. Certainly all the senses were brought into play; this was realized from the outset and emphasized by Gagliano.[2] But there was still no clear-cut difference between the technique which attempted to portray the workings of the imagination in a character, or the reactions to particular circumstances in a plot by means of the novel treatment of dissonance involving the peculiar freedom of the vocal parts, the posturing and devices to entrance the eye, and the intellectual part, the action in which the story unfolds. Before 1637 the real aria and recitative were beginning to take on their characteristics in which the aria represented the emotions and the recitative the factual narrative. But originally, just as our metaphysical poets made little distinction between fact and fiction, playing the one off to reinforce the other, the distinction between recitative and formal aria was not so marked; recitative merged into arioso with only an occasional strophic song or set aria as in Monteverdi's *Orfeo*.

The philosophical tendencies of the time made a marked distinction between fact and fiction, 'between what you felt as a human being, or as a poet and what you thought as a man of sense, judgment and enlightenment'[3]—the logical outcome of opinion that considered truth as demonstrable by mathematics and consequently anything undemonstrable as untrue. Such a philosophy was bound by implication to affect poetry. For the art of poetry depends upon its suggestive power and falls within the category of the unprovable. In this connexion it is an interesting fact that the late seventeenth-century philosopher Vico should stress the point that poetry by its use of metaphor should have had the most powerful effect on the mind of primitive man. He considered metaphor to be 'most praised when it gives sense and

[1] Père Charles F. Menestrier, *Des Representations en musique anciennes et modernes*, Paris, 1681, p. 95.

[2] Angelo Solerti, op. cit., vol. ii, p. 69: 'come quello nel quale s'unisce ogni più nobil diletto . . . da maniera che, con l'intelletto, vien lusingato in uno stesso tempo ogni sentimento più nobile delle più dilettevoli arti ch'abbia ritrovate l'ingegno umano.'

[3] Basil Willey, *The Seventeenth Century Background*, London, 1946, pp. 87–88. For a discussion of the relations between rationalist philosophy and music, Arthur W. Locke, 'Descartes and Seventeenth century Music', *Musical Quarterly*, vol. xxi, p. 423, October 1935, and L. Racek, 'L'esthétique musicale de Descartes', *La Revue Musicale*, November 1930, no. 109, p. 289.

passion to insensate things, in accordance with the being of animate substances, with capacities measured by their own, namely sense and passion. . . '.[1] It is hard to say whether Metastasio could have had any such theory in mind when he wrote his innumerable metaphor arias. But it is significant that these men were contemporaries and friends in Naples, where the powers of poetry in this sense were being studied afresh not only by Vico, but by Metastasio's patron and master Vincenzo Gravina ' "the thinker" who initiated that dominating movement of the later eighteenth century, which, in northern Europe aimed at setting a real classicism drawn from first-hand familiarity with the Greeks in the place of the pseudo-classicism of the later Renaissance'.[2] However, the result in Venice was a series of verses intended to delight, and ultimately to delight the worst elements of the very cosmopolitan population. Faustini, as early as 1643, complained of the licence allowed poets under the plea of an imitation of nature in the preface to his libretto *L'Egisto*; 'the theatre longs for the means to arouse wonder and delight; sometimes dances, ornaments, and the trappings of royalty deceive the eyes, making beautiful the most misshapen objects'. Dryden established it 'for a rule of practice on the stage, that we are bound to please those whom we pretend to entertain; and that at any price, religion and good manner only excepted', and took pains to limit the extent to which an imitation of nature was permissible.[3] But a rule that made 'delight' the criterion could not effectively check bad taste in less tasteful authors. Music, however, was considered the 'unconscious realization of mathematical proportions'. And 'as the unconscious counting of the soul' Leibniz gave it an intellectual importance denied to poetry. The rules, therefore, which governed the choice of subject and the treatment of librettos were not those which governed other forms of drama.

Following the close parallel between speech and singing, musical theorists evolved formulae in the manner of the rhetorical figures.[4]

[1] Giambattista Vico, *The New Science*, tr. from the third edition by Bergin and Fisch, Cornell University Press, 1948, Bk. 2, ch. 2, sec. 404.

[2] John George Robertson, *Studies in the Genesis of Romantic Theory in the Eighteenth Century*, Cambridge, 1923, p. 54.

[3] John Dryden, Dedication to *Examen Poeticum*, 1645. *Essays*, ed. W. P. Ker, Oxford, 1900, vol. ii, p. 7.

[4] Giulio Caccini, *Le Nuove Musiche*, Florence, 1614 ed. Ai discretti Lettori: '. . si rende piacevole, licenzioso e arioso, si come nel parlar comune la eloquenza alle figure e ai colori rettorici assimiglierei i passaggi, i trilli e gli altri simili ornamenti, che spaziamente in ogni effetto si possono tal'ora introdurre . . . .'

Patterns, by the middle of the century, began to play a large part in the technique of composition. Contemporary textbooks dealt with such tricks as inversion, diminution, imitation, and the extra-musical ideas, abstractions much in keeping with the philosophical ideas of the time. The composer in this way was able to put across his ideas in a concise and clear form capable of rational explanation. Later the intellectual meaning of these musical figures reached its most masterful exponent in J. S. Bach. The soul was moved by the affections, represented in music by a note pattern. Caccini explains how he 'endeavoured the imitation of the conceit of the words, seeking out the chords more or less passionate according to the meaning of them'.[1] But these patterns were not fixed. The same figure, depending upon its musical content, could reproduce different affections and was often dependent upon the literary title at the head of the piece for its explanation. It was the basis for development, an abstraction made concrete in music.[2] And because music could realize this abstraction so clearly, philosophers were intrigued by its properties and gave them such earnest attention. As the operatic form crystallized into recitative and aria, the dependence of the extra-musical idea upon the technical figures became very plain. It prevented the new art from becoming a formless opiate that flooded both the eye and ear with a series of luscious sensations.

Operas were written 'in such a way that, both the mind and the most elevated feelings could be enchanted at the same time by the most delightful arts the wit of man could invent'.[3] The poets who wrote the librettos in Venice were very conscious of the ease with which public entertainment can become a simple titillation of bad taste. Very often they fell into the trap. It is therefore important to remember that the visual aids to the dramatic were based on a reasonable foundation which theorists were at pains to explain. The machines

[1] Giulio Caccini, *Le Nuove Musiche*, Florence, 1601. Ai lettori: 'Ho sempre procurata l'imitazione de i concetti delle parole, ricercando quelle corde più o meno affetuoso, secondo i sentimenti di esse.'

[2] Much light is thrown on the patterns and the importance in which they were held by the correspondence between the French philosophers, such as Descartes and Mersenne, with Netherlands musicians in Jonckbloet et Land, *Musique et Musiciens au XVIIᵉ siècle*, Leyden, 1882. The Dutch composer Bannius carried the theory of musical figures to extreme lengths. But he writes to William Boswell in 1637 (p. lxiii): 'finis musicae est docere, delectare et movere. Is musico cum oratore communis est: licet aliis mediis musicus quam orator.'

[3] Angelo Solerti, op. cit., vol. ii, p. 69. From Gagliano's preface to *Dafne*, 1608: 'di maniera che, con l'intelletto, vien lusingato in uno stesso tempo ogni sentimento più nobile dalle più dilettevoli arti ch'abbia ritrovato l'ingegno umano.'

of the early periods were technical means to introduce the supernatural into the plot. The scenes in perspective were to lead the senses away from the servitude to the machines along the lines suggested by the set, and then to allow the imagination to play upon the intellect. In the score, the recitative was the means of telling the story, heightened later, in moments of emotion, by the use of orchestra and a freer vocal line, recitativo accompagnato, whilst the aria filled the moments of repose in which the individual character was able to disclose personal reactions. The *bel canto* eventually claimed all the attention and to a point emasculated the performance of its virile dramatic power. But it is important to remember that 'to the Italian music is a means of self-expression, or rather self-intensification'[1] and that the figurative interpretation now allowed to the works of Bach was present in a less developed way in the works of the Venetian stage. In the development of the aria the poet made each verse a variant of one basic affection or, in the embryonic da capo form, he contrived to show both sections as a different side to the original mood. Opera, by its ability to realize what in poetry must remain suggestive only, proved in combination the ideal medium for seventeenth-century artistic ideals.

[1] Edward Dent, *Foundations of English Opera*, Cambridge, 1928, p. 2.

The State of the Stage in Italy by 1637

Our source of knowledge of the classical stage had always been the books of Vitruvius. Although the manuscripts were known in the early part of the fifteenth century at St. Gall, at Monte Cassino and Avignon[1] the first printed edition was published in Rome[2] (1486) through the efforts of Giovanni Sulpicio of Veroli and Pomponio Leto. A further edition followed, printed in Florence (1496), and another from Venice (1497). Commentaries and editions were printed in profusion through the next century. The first illustrated edition came from Venice (1511).[3] The Vitruvius books contained a good deal of information on the theatre, but give us only a slight idea of the ancient stage. The several editors themselves put their own interpretations on the text which, although often plausible, are by no means authoritative. In point of fact there was as much ignorance of stage practice of the ancient world at this time as there was over musical theory as judged by the pundits of the seventeenth century. Passages on music taken from classical authors were discussed and theories were constructed. But the absence of any ancient music itself made it impossible to know exactly how it sounded. Nevertheless, it was the desire for knowledge and the enthusiasm to interpret classical ideas according to contemporary needs that provided the basis for the artistic and scholastic endeavours. In practice the first man to give us a real knowledge of sixteenth-century stage design is Sebastiano Serlio (1475–1554), who collated the various interpretations of Vitruvius and formed a set of rules that are the foundations of stage design as we know it. His book containing rules for the stage appeared first in 1545[4] and was at once translated into French by Jehan Martin under the author's supervision: it was followed by a Dutch translation in turn put into English in 1611.[5] He divides the scenes into three categories, Comical, Tragical,

---

[1] Hélène Leclerc, *Les Origines italiennes de l'architecture théâtrale moderne*, Paris, 1946, pp. 51–52.

[2] *Lucii Vitruvii Pollionis De Architecture libri Decem*, Rome, 1486.

[3] *M. Vitruvius per Jocundum solito castigatior factus cum Figuris et Tabula ut iam legi et intelligi possit*, Venetus, 1511.   [4] Sebastiano Serlio, *Il Secondo Libro de Perspettia*, Paris, 1545.

[5] *The first Book of Architecture, made by Sebastian Serly, entreating of Perspective which is Inspection,*

and Satyrical. The three plates he gives are the prototypes of all that is to follow and influence to an easily recognizable degree the scene designers in Europe throughout the seventeenth century.[1] We have only to compare the Serlio sets (Pls. 2–4*a*), with an example from Torelli's *Venere Gelosa*, Venice, 1644 (Pl. 20*a*), and *Il Trionfo d'Augosto in Egito*, Milan, 1672 (Pl. 4*b*), to notice the similarity in treatment. The tragical set for *Venere Gelosa* and the satyrical for the Milanese stage obviously derive from a study of Serlio's plates. Yet, by the mid-seventeenth century, some of the distinctions between the three types had disappeared, which gave greater scope to the designer unhampered by the originally strict conventions. The distinction, for example, between the tragical and comical is harder to make in Torelli's sets. And thus the conventional requirements of Serlio gradually disappear although in symmetrical design there is little change.

It is important to understand the symbolic intentions of seventeenth-century producers and designers as they differed somewhat from the older ideas. In the operas so much that must pass us by now was clear by implications to a seventeenth-century audience. Imagination was allowed a wider scope and was in consequence more nimble than in later ages. Whenever technical needs are limited convention plays a vital part, and the whole standard of early dramatic performance depended upon the convention employed. For example, Serlio writes, 'Houses for Tragedies, must be made for great personages for that actions of love, strange adventures and cruell murthers (as you read in ancient and moderne Tragedies) happen always in the homes of great Lords, Dukes, Princes and Kings. Therefore in such cases you must make none but stately houses.' And naturally at a time when scenery remained set throughout the piece these conventions affected the character of the plot. A change of scenery could take place in the *intermedii*, considered to have derived from the interludes in classical comedy. And, although there may be little to support this assumption on the part of renaissance dramatists, the *intermedii* took on great

or looking into by shortening of the sight. Translated out of Italian into Dutch, and out of Dutch into English, London, 1611. By Robert Peake. My quotations, compared with the Italian edition of 1551 in the British Museum are from this translation.

[1] A late example of the influence of the set scene is to be found in the opera *Scipione Africano*, Drama per Musica da rappresentarsi in Ferrara nel Teatro di San Stefano, 1669, in which one of the scenes is labelled 'Tragica con Loggie'. This archaic heading is not found in the Venice editions of this opera.

significance as far as the origins of opera are concerned. They contained much of musical as well as scenic interest.[1] For stage practice they are important as the source for the elaborate machines. It was not considered out of place in them, did not in fact infringe upon the unities of the so-called classical practice, if there were several changes of machinery, whereas in the actual play the unities were preserved and the plots built around the three sets with which Serlio deals. In Venetian operatic practice the main plot and the *intermedii* were combined, although later, the intermezzos of Neapolitan opera such as *La serva padrona*, which was acted as an interlude to Pergolesi's own *opera seria Il prigioner superbo*, may be a relic of the ancient practice. This ironing out of distinctions can be traced in the Venetian operas from 1637 onwards.

Serlio's directions were intended for scenes built for specific occasions in the great courts or rooms of Princes. The well-known Teatro Olimpico at Vicenza is the first building designed with a permanent set. Planned originally by Palladio and finished after his death by Scamozzi, it was first opened in 1585 by the members of the Accademia Olympica who performed on 3 March an Italian version of *Oedipus Rex*. The action took place in front of the elegant set. And the three famous streets, themselves the heirs to the labelled compartments from which the characters of Terence emerge in woodcuts of fifteenth-century editions,[2] designed in magnificent perspective, led nowhere. They were not exits. The actors came in from customary doors on either side of the stage. However, it was not long before further development was planned.

Three years later (1588-9) Scamozzi designed the Gonzaga's little theatre at Sabbioneta, an interesting experiment in which he combined the Vicenza streets into long perspective carried forward to the edge of the stage and culminating in the proscenium arch, an innovation which can be dated from this design.[3] Architecturally, the stage had assumed a form recognizable in modern theatres.

The growth of the scene-changing apparatus can again be traced back to Vitruvius, and the earliest-known illustrations come from

---

[1] S. Towneley Worsthorne, 'The Origins of Italian Opera', *The Month*, August 1950.

[2] For example, the woodcuts of the 1493 Treschel edition of Terence, an illustration of which is published as plate xiii in Leclerq, op. cit., or the Venice edition of Palutus, 1518, given in *Theatre Notebook*, vol. iii, no. 4, 1949, p. 50.

[3] Franco Barbieri, *Vincenzo Scamozzi*, Vicenza, 1952, pl. 26.

PLATE 2

S. Serlio, *Il Secondo Libro di Perspettiva*, Venice 1551, p. 20 v.
Della Scena Comica.

PLATE 3

Ibid., p. 29 v. *Della Scena Tragica*

PLATE 4

a

Ibid., p. 30 v. *Della Scena Satyrica*

b

Il Trionfo d'Augosto in Egito (from the libretto Milan, 1672)

Antonio di San Gallo (1485–1546)[1] who explained, as he thought, classical intentions. On either side of the main set were built two rooms, actually part of the stage from which the actors entered. In front of these rooms were triangular constructions that turned according to the three types of scenery required. At once one notices the discrepancy between the set scene of Serlio and the machines of San Gallo. The explanation is that architects of the day made of Vitruvius's obscure texts what they could and were themselves evolving technique that they liked to mask with the respectability of a classical past. An edition of Vitruvius, edited by Daniel Barbaro (1556), shows these *scenae versatiles*; such erections were put behind the openings that Palladio later prolonged into his street perspectives. They were built to revolve. By this means notice was given to the audience that the place in the scene had changed. This was an adequate method so long as the actors played on a fore-stage using the set as a background. But directly the proscenium arch moved forward it was not so satisfactory. And it must be remembered that on the operatic stage the actors stood within the scenery, not using it as a kaleidoscopic background as was the habit during the seventeenth and eighteenth centuries at the play. Scamozzi brought further improvements into his Sabbioneta design by leaving openings down the sides of the stage, not false as in those of Serlio and Palladio, but actual exits behind the houses which the players could use and thus obviated the necessity for a *scena versatilis*. Vasari's plan for the theatre in his ideal city,[2] which anticipates Sabbattini's detailed treatise,[3] developed from this improvement. He gives plans of two-sided flats that pivot at the angle, an adaptation of the old *scena versatilis*. This practice offered a variation noted also by Sabbattini, whereby a change of scene could be effected through drawing one of a pair of two-sided flats in front of the other. When not required the movable flat fitted behind one of another pair as will be seen in the figure (p. 22).

The second type of scene, used for the back of the stage, the *scena ductilis*, was considered fully by the Frenchman Guillaume Philandrier (1506–65) in his annotations of Vitruvius in 1544.[4] He describes a

---

[1] See plate v in Leclerc, op. cit., from a design in the Uffizi Library, Florence.
[2] Giorgio Vasari, *La città ideale del Cav^re*. *Vasari*, State Archives, Florence, 1548.
[3] Niccolò Sabbattini, *La Practica di fabricar scene e machine ne' teatri*, Ravenna, 1638. French tr., Neuchâtel, 1942.
[4] *Gulielmi Philandri Castilionii Gallicivis Ro. In Decem libros M. Vitruvii Pollionis*, Rome, 1554.

simple construction which runs on grooves to form a back-cloth or two flats which when closed have a similar function, but which, when drawn back to either side of the stage, disclose a scene in perspective familiar to us from the designs of Inigo Jones.[1] And this became the normal method in Venice. It is illustrated in the plan for

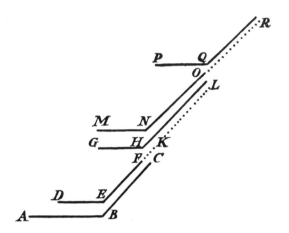

SS. Giovanni e Paolo. The spaces marked *Strade* in the wings were used as exits from which we can gather that the whole stage was used by the cast and could be regulated for size by the perspective shutters. It may well be that it could be made to stretch as far as the back wall of the theatre[2] for particularly crowded scenes. The practice introduced later of acting at the footlights is much complained of by Algarotti, who is always urging a return to seventeenth-century customs. 'The actors', he writes, 'instead of being so brought forward, ought to be thrown back at a certain distance from the spectator's eye, and stand within the scenery of the stage, in order to make a part of that pleasing illusion for which all dramatic exhibitions are calculated.'[3]

It is possible then to say that at the opening of the seventeenth century the requirements for stage scenery were fully understood by the architects of the day. The scenes in perspective, whether a room, a street, or a garden, which are found in every opera for certainly a hundred and fifty years after the opening of the first public opera-house in 1637, resemble each other in conventional form as closely as the layout of one libretto came to resemble another later in the century. An

[1] Lansdowne MS. 1171. (B.M.)
[2] The theatre at Caserta is an eighteenth-century example of this practice.
[3] Count Francesco Algarotti, *An Essay on the Opera*, London, 1767, p. 97.

international school of stage architects grew up as companions to the itinerant Italian composers of the day.

Jacomo Torelli, the first great designer of scenery for operas who was employed in Venice from an early date, and whose fame led Mazerin to invite him to Paris in the ill-fated attempt to introduce Italian opera into the French court, was really concerned more with the invention of new machinery, apparatus to man the chariots, the tackle to fly gods and monsters from one part of the stage to another, fountains, rivers, and machinery to effect a transformation scene, those marvels in fact which went under the heading of *machine*, were his concern rather than the decorated wings and back-cloth. The technique for machines developed rapidly during the seventeenth century. And Venice was able to give the lead to Europe through her many public opera-houses. Sabbattini collected into one book[1] the various methods. And it is as a detailed summary that his book is valuable to us.

The early plans for the auditorium show the semicircle as the most usual shape. Gallo and Pirovano[2] give a most interesting design for the auditorium that shows not only banked rows of seats round an arena but also two rows of what appear to be boxes but may be corridors with arches. The effect, from the plan, is of a small semicircular Colosseum. However, some of the theatres kept the oblong, conforming to the usual shape of the rooms that were converted for single performances. At court entertainments the important personages sat in the body of the hall, in the *platea* or stalls, whilst behind them in their degrees were ranged the officials and lesser men and women.[3] But the *Teatro Farnese*, the largest theatre in seventeenth-century Italy, constructed according to the plans of Aleotti (1546–1636) for Ranuccio I of Parma in 1618–19, has the first U-shaped plan for an auditorium; a plan that, with modifications, has been in use in opera houses ever since. No doubt the evolution of the auditorium with its trials and experiments would have been well illustrated in the Venetian opera-houses, had we more than the one plan, now in the Sir John Soane Museum, from which to judge. For it was in this direction that a specifically public theatre would stimulate an architect's imagination, to combine the economic necessity of packing the house with as

---

[1] Niccolò Sabbattini, op. cit.

[2] *Di Lucio Vitruvio Pollione de Architectura Libri Decem Traducti de latino in Vulgare affigurati*, Como, 1521, facing p. lxxxiii. (By Augustino Gallo and Alvisio da Pirovano.)

[3] Niccolò Sabbattini, op. cit., pp. 55–57.

many seats as possible and yet to ensure that the stage could be seen from all angles and, in addition, to provide satisfactory acoustics. The solution adopted was the elliptical auditorium with the sides built up into tiers of boxes.

The original idea of a box to segregate important officials can be traced to an illustration in the Trechsel edition of Terence of 1493. Here the Aediles occupy a privileged position to the left of the stage, and the public sits in three tiers around the auditorium.[1] Boxes as we know them existed from the outset in Venetian theatres. But for early designs we are dependent upon Bologna. An open-air temporary theatre of 1636 was provided with three rows of boxes and by 1639 the Teatro della Sala[2] had five.

From our knowledge of the state of stage design and architecture in the past, we can sum up accurately the position of the stage in Venice by 1637. Side wings, both the *scena versatilis* and *scena ductilis*, would have been used; back-cloths and relieves of the type familiar to us from Jacobean masques were developed to the maximum complexity; the stage was used in its entirety as a frame for the actors instead of as a background; the use of a curtain was established. We know from an account in the scenario that it was used in the first opera-house in San Cassiano from its opening on 6 May 1637. The position of the orchestra in the early days is not clear, although it quickly gained its present place. Sabbattini advises that it shall be put at the sides. Probably it was placed, divided if necessary, out of the way of the stage-hands. But it must be remembered that Sabbattini was not considering the opera-houses. A design of Antonio San Gallo[3] shows the orchestra in front of the stage. But discussion on this point must be reserved for a later chapter.

Elaborate mechanical effects were gained by quite simple means. The chapter-headings in Sabbattini's book[4] show the machines available to him. And the scenario for *Andromeda* of 1637 gives an account of the effect produced on the audience which, better than anything else, will conjure up the marvels which were to hand. The novel experiment of a commercial entertainment inaugurated by Manelli and Ferrari dates from this production. Certainly the effect was so profound

[1] Hélène Leclerc, op. cit., pl. xlix.
[2] Corrado Ricci, *Teatri di Bologna*, Bologna, 1888. Plate facing p. 32.
[3] *The Mask*, vol. ii, 1925, pl. ii.   [4] See Appendix II.

that opera became an economic proposition at once. The importance of *Andromeda*, however, lies in its chronological position, not in its superior merits, since works soon to follow in the Teatro Novissimo were more elaborate. But the description deserves a full quotation,[1] since it was the first of such entertainments.

The curtain disappears. The scene was entirely sea. In the distance was a view of water and rocks so contrived that its naturalness (although feigned) moved the spectators to doubt whether they were in a theatre or on a real sea-shore. The scene was quite dark except for the light given by a few stars which disappeared one after another, giving place to Aurora who came to make the prologue. She was dressed entirely in cloth of silver with a shining star on her brow, and appeared inside a very beautiful cloud which sometimes grew large and sometimes small [Sabbattini, Bk. ii, ch. 46, explains the technique], and oh lovely surprise! circled across the sky on the stage. Meantime the scene grew light as day for the prologue, sung divinely by Signora Madelena Manelli from Rome, after which one heard a very sweet symphony from the most polished instrumentalists, assisted by the author of the opera[2] with his miraculous theorbo. . . . Then Juno came out on a golden car drawn by her pea-cocks, blazing in a coat of cloth of gold with a superb variety of jewels on her head or in her crown. To the wondering delight of the spectators the car turned from right to left as it pleased her. Mercury appeared before her. This personage was and was not in a machine. He was, since flying, it is impossible not to admit it; he was not, since one saw no other machine but that of a flying body. He appeared adorned in his customary garments with a blue mantle that waved loosely from his shoulders. Juno was excellently played by Signora Francesca Angeletti of Assisi and Mercury exquisitely by Signor Don Annibale Graselli from Città di Castello. In a moment one saw the scene change from a sea scape to a wood so natural that it carried our eyes to the life to real snowy heights, real flowering countryside, a regal spreading wood (reale intrecciatura del Bosco) and unfeigned melting of water. Andromeda appeared with a following of twelve damsels dressed as nymphs. Andromeda's dress was of the colour of fire of inestimable value, that of the nymphs was white, flesh colour and gold. Andromeda was wonderfully represented by her who did the pro-logue. The scene turned in a moment from the wood to the sea scape. Neptune appeared and Mercury came out to meet him in a wonderful machine. Neptune was on a great silver shell drawn by four sea horses and a sky blue mantle covered him. A large beard came down to his breast and a long shock of hair wreathed with sea-weed hung down to his shoulders. His crown was made as a pyramid tossed with pearls. This part was played excellently by Signor Francesco Manelli of Tivoli, composer of the music of the opera. Prometheo came from the bosom of the sea

---

[1] See Appendix III for the original description.

[2] At this time a work was described as a rule on the title-page as a *Dramma* or *Favole in musica*. But the authors call them familiarly 'questa mia povera opera', and contemporary accounts start at an early date to speak of 'opera' as an isolated term. It is interesting to see that the librettist is called the author, 'l'Autore dell' Opera'.

dressed in silver scales with a great shock of hair and a blue beard. Signor Giò Battista Bisucci from Bologna served as this very gentle personage. Here to end the act they sung firstly a madrigal for many voices, behind the scene, concerted with different instruments; and then three very beautiful youths, dressed as Loves, came out to make a most graceful dance as an Intermezzo. The speed of the movements of these children sometimes made people doubt if they might not have wings on their shoulders or indeed on their feet. To the tune of a sweet melody of instruments Astrea appeared in the sky and Venus in the sea; one in a silver cloud and the other in her shell drawn by swans. Astrea was dressed in the colour of the sky, a flaming sword in her right hand; Venus in sea colour with a gold cloak clinging to her shoulders. Astrea was gracefully played by Signor Girolamo Medici a Roman, and Venus most sweetly by Signor Anselmo Marconi a Roman. The scene changed to a woodland, and Andromeda came out with her train. Six of her ladies, for joy at killing a boar, did a light and wonderful ballet with such varied and different weaving of paces that truly one was able to call it a leaping labyrinth. It was the invention of the celebrated Venetian dancer Signor Giò Battista Balbi. Suddenly, from beneath the stage arose the magician Astarco as a ghost [Sabbattini, ch. 56]. This personage was clad entirely in a long deep gold coat with hair and a long beard white as snow. As a sorcerer's sceptre, he held a wand in his right hand. This character was worthily represented by him who played Neptune. The sky opened and in a burst of light one saw sitting on a stately throne Jove and Juno. Jove was covered by a starry cloak and on his hair was set a crown of rays and a thunderbolt in his right hand. He who performed Proteo played this part divinely. Here, to finish the act, another madrigal for many voices was sung within firstly concerted with different instruments. And then twelve wood nymphs made, as an intermezzo, a very eccentric and tasteful ballet of movements and gestures. There were no eyes that did not weep the passing of this dance. The above-mentioned dancer Signor Giò Battista Balbi was the inventor. The scene changed to the sea-shore. In tune to a most sweet harmony of different instruments a very beautiful machine appeared from one side of the scene with Astrea and Venus upon it. It turned to the right and left as these goddesses most pleased. Opposite them Mercury came out and, the sky opening, sat in the middle. This little scene had a most wonderful effect for the quantity of machines and for the successive arrangements of silent characters and movement (on the stage). In a flash the sea scene became a superb palace. It was a good sight to see a well laid out and constructed building suddenly born from rough stone and coarse sand. This represented the royal palace of Andromeda from which came Ascalà a knight. His clothes exceeded in value and beauty those of all the rest. He was dressed in the Turkish style.[1] This unhappy character, with a thousand charms of heaven, was played by him who took Mercury. Regretfully the palace disappeared and we saw the scene entirely of sea with Andromeda bound to a rock. The sea monster came out. This animal was made with such beautiful cunning that, although not real, he put people

---

[1] An interesting study of the use of foreign clothes in ballet (and their political significance) is to be found in Marcel Paquet, *Les Étrangers dans les divertissements de la cour*, Paris, 1932. In music such dances as the moresca testify, at an early date, to non-European influence.

in terror. Except for the act of tearing to pieces and devouring he did everything as if alive and breathing. Perseus arrived on Pegasus, and with three blows of a lance and five with a rapier he overthrew the monster and killed it. This character was dressed in white with a great crest on his helmet. His flying steed had a plume with the same device on its head. This character was played angelically by him who took Ascalà. The sky opened and one saw Jove and Juno in glory and other divinities. This great machine descended to the ground to the accompaniment of a concerto of voices and instruments truly from heaven. The two heroes, joined to each other, it conducted to the sky. Here the royal and ever worthy occasion had an end.

From the quick changes of scene necessary we can judge the type of stage-craft necessary. Probably the Teatro San Cassiano employed the *scena versatilis* with its two sides, for only two basic sets were used; some kind of 'relievo' would give the effect of a vast sea from which the monster could emerge. We shall see how the opera plots gained, in complexity, and how, in a very few years, the number of changes in scenery was vastly increased. But there were few fundamental novelties. As is often the case, the formal theory is stated after the practical experiments have proved themselves. Fabricio Motta,[1] forty years later, gives formal instruction for the convenient size of boxes and how to arrange the seating to ensure the best views. Yet it seems unlikely that Venetians, attending the opera almost daily, had not solved that problem themselves. The next advance in stage design is to be found in Troili's book,[2] in which he gives directions for oblique scenes, wings that slant towards the back of the stage and which are an added help to the perspective. But in practice this type of scene had been used in Venice for the Teatro San Giovanni e Paolo.

The knowledge of what was common practice in Italy by 1637 makes it easier to understand the workings of the elaborate sets that we shall find in Venetian theatres. For it is clear that designers had a tradition at their finger tips with which to assuage the sudden thirst for operatic entertainment. And the convention, older and stronger than the tentative attempts of the new art, in some measure regulated the form which at any rate the libretto was subsequently to take. Economic pressure ensured that maximum use was made of the elaborate machines and sets already in hand, so that the poets kept their imagination within the bounds of the opera-house store-rooms.

[1] Fabricio Casini Motta, *Trattato sopra la struttura de Theatri e scene*, &c., Guastalla, 1676.
[2] Giulio Troili, *Paradossi per practicare la perspettiva senza saperla*, Bologna, 1683.

Venetian Theatres

The Baedeker of his day, Padre Coronelli, includes a map in his *Guida de' Forestieri*.[1] The edition of 1700 marks seven theatres. But from 1637 they were a mushroom growth. And, in fact, by the turn of the century some, the names of which we know, were already derelict and thus have no place in his Guide. The Teatro Novissimo visited by Evelyn, for example, is not marked on the map, for Coronelli shows only those in use for the current year. But for convenience sake his omissions have been corrected on the map reproduced in this book.

Usually an opera-house was called after the parish in which it was situated. The first building to be used for such a purpose was the theatre in San Cassiano, called 'il nuovo' to distinguish it from an old ruin near by built for the performance of plays in 1556 by Palladio. The new theatre had been ruined once by fire in 1629, but was entirely redesigned for the performance of Manelli's *Andromeda* first given there on 6 March 1637. It remained open as an opera-house until 1695, after which plays were produced there as well.[2] The Parisian journal *Mercure Galant*, some fifty years later describes it as having five rows of boxes, with thirty-one to each row.[3] But it is impossible to state whether these were not a later addition. It is possible that the first opera-house should have been constructed with boxes, although, until entertainment was organized on a public basis, there was little need for any such segregation. For it is only after such places came to be considered almost as second homes, so to speak, that the convenience of a proprietory right was felt necessary. Certainly the Teatro della Sala at Bologna had five tiers of boxes in 1639. An engraving of the interior is the first illustration extant of the appearance of an opera-house.[4] Bologna quickly developed its own opera very much on the lines of the Venetians: in fact, productions often went from the one town to the other.

[1] Vincenzo Coronelli, *Guida de' Forestieri per succintamente osservare tutto il più reguardevole nella Città di Venetia*, Venice, 1700.

[2] Taddeo Wiel, *Teatri musicali veneziani del settecento*, Venice, 1879, p. xlii.

[3] *Mercure Galant*, 1683, p. 289.

[4] Corrado Ricci, *I teatri di Bologna*, Bologna, 1888, facing p. 32.

The second opera-house in Venice was built in SS. Giovanni e Paolo and opened on 20 January 1639. It remained in use until 1748, although there were periods of eclipse in its fortunes. Like San Cassiano it had been used for plays, but appears to have been rebuilt entirely of stone 'a dar grido alla Virtù de' Cantati'.[1] The plan of this theatre, now in the Sir John Soane Museum, London, is a unique document,[2] invaluable as a means of showing how quickly theatrical architecture developed owing to the popularity of these public entertainments. Mlle Leclerc inclines to date this drawing at 1655.[3] Wiel mentions a new theatre for 1654.[4] But neither of these authorities gives a reference in support of the dates. Bonlini states categorically that the theatre was transported in 1639 a little distance from an older site under the authority of Giovanni Grimani and rebuilt entirely of stone 'come si trova al presente'.[5] And he is writing a century later. Tassini, the most reliable of modern Venetian topographers, agrees with this date.[6] Neither makes reference to a further building, and Ivanovich[7] states categorically that there was no new theatre. Mlle Leclerc assumes that the interior of the theatre is later than 1678, on account of a manuscript note on the plan in which the architect describes himself as 'Ingiegniero dell' Ecc^{mo} Sud^{tto} nel Teatro di Sto. Gio. Grisostomo', itself not finished until that date. But this indicates only that the plan, not the theatre, is of a later date. We cannot be sure that the same architect designed both theatres. It seems more likely that the drawing was made as a matter of interest.

It is interesting to compare the size of SS. Giovanni e Paolo with the older Teatro Farnese at Parma and the new theatre at the Tuileries inaugurated in 1662 with Cavalli's *Ercole Amante*,[8] which is considerably larger. The comparison will put right the false view which sees the new public opera as a popular art catering for a different class of

---

[1] Giovanni Bonlini, *Le glorie della poesia e della musica*, Venice, 1730, p. 37.

[2] It is in an album of thirty-six designs entered under *Teatro di Tor di Nona del C. Carlo Fontana, de Roma, Firenze, Siena, Fano*. Most of the drawings are signed by Fontana. There is only one plan from Venice, which seems to have been included by mistake. (Pl. 7.)

[3] Hélène Leclerc, *Les Origines italiennes de l'architecture théâtrale moderne*, Paris, 1946, pp. 147, 199.

[4] Taddeo Wiel, op. cit., p. xliii.   [5] Giovanni Bonlini, op. cit., p. 20.

[6] Giuseppe Tassini, *Curiosità Veneziane*, Venice, 1933, 6th ed., p. 75.

[7] Christoforo Ivanovich, *Minerva sulla Tavolina*, Venice, 1681, p. 399: 'Il terzo à Santi Gio: e Paolo, fù aperto l'anno 1638 (M.V.). . . . Hà servito sempre, e tuttavia continua nell' Opere Musicali.'

[8] Henry Prunières, *L'Opéra italien en France avant Lulli*, Paris, 1913, pp. 218–19.

audience from the court theatre; as an art which catered for the un-tutored mass of the population. The Republic was as aristocratic, the nobility in many cases more ancient and as consciously privileged as any in Europe. And it would be wrong to associate the great names of Venetian history with a merchant class, representing a new force in social life. The Grimani, Giustiniani, and other families who owned and managed the opera-houses were part of the great network of relationships whose tastes and fancies shaped the geography of Europe. These operatic ventures must be compared with the Opera of the Nobility or the Concerts of Antient Music in eighteenth-century London, the organization of which was actively managed by members of the great English families. The opera was a sophisticated form of entertainment from its early history: it required a more intimate setting than the great theatre at Parma. Venice was ideally situated to provide the necessary atmosphere, because no one family dominated the political scene and the topographical circumstances of the city—large tracts of land were not available—made it a greater convenience to build small theatres; and private theatricals on that scale had had a long tradition. Even opera itself may have flourished, as Schrade[1] suggests, in private performances many years before the opening of the public opera-house.

A comparison of the two theatres, both as regards the size of the stages and the auditoriums, shows the one as a place fit for the regal court, designed to accommodate not only the royal suite and privileged guests, but the host of courtiers and servants in attendance, without which court life cannot function, whereas the other is built for the closed exclusive society of an oligarchy.

	Teatro Farnese	SS. Giovanni e Paolo
Over-all length	286 ft. 4 in.	128 ft. 5 in.
Over-all breadth	105 ft. 7 in.	61 ft. 4 in.
Height	72 ft. 3 in.	35 ft. 5 in. (from floor to ceiling in auditorium)
Stage depth	13 ft. 4 in.	72 ft.
Width at the proscenium arch .	39 ft. 5 in.	32 ft.
Length of auditorium		41 ft. 10 in.
Breadth of the centre boxes		5 ft. 7 in.
Breadth of the rest of boxes		4 ft. 6 in.
Width of the corridor circling boxes . . .		3 ft. 7 in.

[1] Leo Schrade, *Monteverdi*, New York, 1950, p. 313.

	Teatro Farnese	SS. Giovanni e Paolo
Width of the orchestra pit at centre	. . .	9 ft. 2 in.
Length of the orchestra pit . .	. .	4 ft. 7 in.
Width between orchestra and pit .	. .	5 ft. 7 in.

An interesting detail in the construction of the Venetian theatre is the sloping ceiling designed to provide a sounding-board above the fore-stage. The staircases leading above and below the stage, placed at the back of the theatre, allow the mechanics to reach the quantity of complex machinery illustrated in plates 8 and 10.

The third opera-house to be opened in Venice was in San Moisè. It was an old theatre site that originally belonged to the Giustiniani of San Barnaba family and later returned to them after passing first to the Zane of San Stin family. As an opera-house it dated from 1640, opening with Monteverdi's *Arianna*. After a fire in 1668 it was rebuilt but considered small, holding eight hundred persons, with only two rows of boxes.[1] Later, the Tuscan Resident tells of 'l'opera in musica con certe figurine di nuova invenzione'[2] for the carnival of 1679–80. But by 1685 it had regained its human cast. Although it had no continuous history as a theatre, it was still in use as such in 1846 when Rossini's *Torvaldo e Dorlisia* was produced there. It then became a carpenter's shop until 1872 when it reopened as a puppet-theatre, remaining open as such until the first years of this century.

The fourth opera-house, the Teatro Novissimo, has a particular interest for Englishmen, from its connexion with John Evelyn. It opened on 14 January 1641, as a wooden theatre, but was destroyed by fire in 1647 and later became the site for the famous *Cavallerizza*, or riding-school. The eight operas performed in this theatre were famous for the sets designed by Torelli, many of which were engraved and published in contemporary librettos. The first opera to be given there, *La Finta Pazza*, was produced in Paris in 1645. Torelli designed the sets for both productions. The elaborate spectacle presented at this theatre is preserved in the illustrated scenarios printed for *Il Bellerofonte* (1642) and *Venere Gelosa* (1644) which, with Evelyn's account of the opera *Ercole in Lidia* by Giovanni Rovetta (1645), gives us an excellent picture of the contemporary scene.[3]

[1] Taddeo Wiel, *I teatri musicali veneziani del Settecento*, Venice, 1897, p. xliii.
[2] Mathias Teglia, Arch. di Stato, Florence, Arch. Mediceo, *Lettere dei Residenti a Ven.*, Filza 3040, c. 827, in Molmenti, *La storia di Venezia*, Bergamo, 1908, iii. 227, n. 3.
[3] *Memoirs of John Evelyn*, ed. W. Bray, London, 1819, vol. i, p. 191, Ascension Week 1645.

This night, having with my Lord Bruce taken our places before,[1] we went to the Opera where comedies and other plays are represented in recitative music by the most excellent musicians vocal and instrumental, with a variety of scenes painted and contrived with no less art of perspective, and machines for flying in the aire, and other wonderful motions; taken together it is one of the most magnificent and expensive diversions the wit of men can invent. The history was Hercules in Lydia, the scenes changed thirteen times. The famous voices, Anna Rencia, a Roman, and reputed the best treble of women; but there was an eunuch who in my opinion surpassed her; also a Genoeze that sang an incomparable bass. This held us by the eyes and ears till two in the morning.

And then follows one of those rare descriptions that enliven research with the power of an uncommonly human story. For Evelyn remained about Venice for some months and writes for January 1646:[2]

the diversion which cheefely tooke me up was three noble operas,[3] where were excellent voices and Musiq, the most celebrated of which was the famous Anna Rencha, whom we invited to a fish dinner after four daies in Lent, when they had given over at the theatre. Accompanied by an eunuch whom she brought with her, she entertained us with rare musiq, both of them singing to an harpsichord. It growing late, a gentleman of Venice, came for her to show her the gallys, now ready to sayle for Candia. This entertainment produced a second, given by the English Consul of the merchants, inviting us to his hous, where he had the Genoeze, the most celebrated bass in Italy, who was one of the late opera band. This diversion held us so late at night that conveying a gentlewoman, who had supped with us, to her gondola at the usual place of landing, we were shot at by two carbines from out another gondola in which was a noble Venetian and his courtezan unwilling to be disturbed which made us run in and fetch other weapons, not knowing what the matter was, till we were informed on the danger we might incur by pursuing it further.

The parish of SS. Apostoli, in which the fifth theatre was built, provides little in the way of descriptive documents to add to our knowledge. There appear to have been two sites for the building. Bonlini assures us that the parish never possessed a formal or secure theatre.[4]

---

[1] The need to procure seats in advance is urged by the *Mercure Galant*, in connexion with a later theatre, S. Salvatore. 'Il faut retenir les Chaises du Parterre deux jours auparavant, à cause de la grande affluence du monde qui s'y trouve' (March 1683).

[2] *Memoirs of John Evelyn*, ed. W. Bray, London, 1819, vol. i, pp. 203 seqq.

[3] The operas to be seen during Evelyn's stay were: *La Doriclea*. Text, Gio. Faustini; music, Cavalli. T. San Cass: *Ercole in Lidia*. Text, M. Bisaccioni; music, G. Rovetta. T. Nov: *Il Bellerofonte*. Text, V. Nolfi; music, Fr. Sacrati. SS. G. e P. Text slightly altered for 1642 production: *Il Titone*. Text, Faustini; music, Cavalli. T. San Cass: *Romolo e Remo*. Text, G. Strozzi; music, Cavalli. SS. G. e P.

[4] Giovanni Bonlini, op. cit., p. 23: 'Quivi veramente non s'è mai veduto alcun teatro formale, e stabile . . . Primieramente in una casa assai capace di Ca' Bellagno, posta in Calle de' Proverbi

PLATE 5

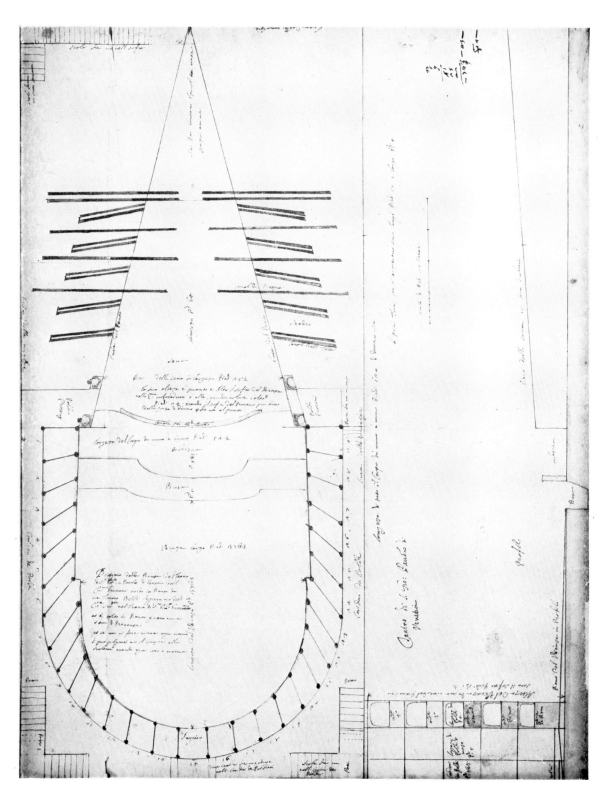

SS. Giovanni e Paolo (1639–1748)

One of the buildings seems to have been of a fair size and remained open from 1649 to 1688. (Allacci gives the closing date as 1687,[1] whilst Ivanovich puts it as early as 1652.)[2] But the other must have been well below the customary Venetian standards.

S. Appolinare, a theatre that owed its short life to Luigi Dandolo, a Procurator of St. Mark's, and Marcantonio Correr, both influential noblemen, opened as the sixth opera-house in 1651. Nine operas were produced there before it closed in 1657.[3] A tenth was produced there in 1660, 'La pazzia in Trono, ovvero Caligula delirante, per vertuosa recreazione delli Signori Accademici Imperturbabili'. Galvani[4] considers that Cavalli set the music for the prologue and intermedii only, and therefore gives it no place as an opera proper. Nevertheless, on the title-page it is called an 'opera di stile recitativo', and it was quite usual for academies to take over disused houses that served admirably for the purpose of private theatricals. The origins of the seventh theatre S. Salvatore are obscure. Some authorities speak of a comedy being performed there in 1622.[5] Bonlini, too, hints at previous origins.[6] It is the oldest opera-house still in use, and opened in 1661 under the direction of the great family of Vendramin. Under various names it has remained a playhouse until the present day, going, since 1875, by the name of the Teatro Goldoni. As an opera-house it opened in 1661 under the direction of the Vendramin of Santa Fosca. It remained open, apart from 1675, throughout the century, giving performances of sixty-seven operas as well as comedies. The Mercure Galant[7] speaks of it as 'fort grand, fort beau, tout paint et doré de neuf, et des plus considérables de Venise. Il contient cinq rangs de palcs, trente trois à chaque rang.' It was entirely restored by Gasparo Torelli before a performance in 1685.

The theatre Ai Saloni is an example of a building put up for a few

o sia Calle larga, dove l'anno 1688 fu sentito l'ultimo Drama intitolato la Floridea, e poi in Calle dell' Oca in un Maggazzino mediocre, dove anche a' giorni nostri si sono rappresentate Comedie, e l'anno 1707 si recitò in musica Prassitele in Gnido.'

[1] Leone Allacci, *Dramaturgia*, Venice, 1755, p. 366.
[2] Christoforo Ivanovich, *Minerva sulla Tavolina*, Venice, 1681, in catalogue.
[3] Giovanni Bonlini, op. cit., p. 59.
[4] Livio-Niso Galvani, *I teatri musicali di Venezia nel sec. XVII*, Milan, 1878.
[5] Giuseppe Tassini, op. cit., p. 690.
[6] Giovanni Bonlini, op. cit., p. 63: 'Questo Teatro, dopo un grave incendio, poco prima sofferto, ridotto a miglior struttura, subito si riapre, non già come prima, alle insipidezze d' Istrioni, ma alle melodie degli Orfei.'
[7] *Mercure Galant*, March 1683, p. 271.

performances. Ivanovich says that it had no complete rows of boxes.[1]
The members of the Academy to whom it belonged had a few facing
the stage, and evidently entertained themselves with operas from
1650. But the first performance which, at their own expense, they
opened to the public in 1670 was *Adelaide*. The impresario Francesco
Santurini who ran the San Moisè Theatre launched a new project in
1676 by renting a house in the parish of S. Angelo from the Marcello
and Cappello families for seven years for the production of operas.
When the lease had expired, it returned to the owners of the property
who carried on the work, giving forty-three new operas by 1700.
Later it was used for comedies, and towards 1800 it fell into ruins. The
original theatre had five rows of boxes with twenty-nine to each row.[2]

However, the theatre built in S. Giovanni Gristostomo outshone
in magnificence anything that had gone before. Built in 1678 by the
architect Tomaso Bezzi for Giovanni Carlo and Vincenzo Grimani,[3] it
was the grandest of the seventeenth-century Venetian opera-houses.
Bonlini says that:

it was built within the space of a few months above the ruins of an old building
already destroyed by fire with that magnificence appropriate to the house of
Grimani. It was once the habitual dwelling of the famous Marco Polo who lived at
the end of the thirteenth century, renowned in every age for his far distant travels.
Thus, from a pile of memorable ashes one saw, almost unexpectedly in this great
capital and true kingdom of marvels, arise this real phoenix of theatres to the glory
of poetry and music, which, with the vastness of its superb structure, was able to
rival the pomp of ancient Rome and which, with the magnificence of its more than
regal dramatic display, has now gained the applause and esteem of the whole world.[4]

An account is included, too, in the *Mercure Galant*.[5] We are told that
it was built in three to four months,

le plus beau, et le plus riche de la ville. La Salle où sont les Spectateurs, est en-
vironnée de cinq rangs de Palcs les uns sur les autres, trente et un à chaque rang. Ils
sont enrichis d'Ornemens de Sculpture en bosse et en relief, tous dorez, représentans
diférentes sortes de Vases antiques, Coquillages, Mussles, Roses, Rosettes, Fleurons,
Feuillages et autres enrichissemens. Au dessous et entre chacun de ces Palcs, sont

[1] Christoforo Ivanovich, op. cit., p. 400.   [2] *Mercure Galant*, March 1683, p. 283.
[3] Heirs of the previous Grimani who were responsible for SS. Giovanni e Paolo. Although this
architect has been called Belli to date, it is likely that the 'll' in the plan of the theatre should read
as 'zz', for it appears in no similar form in any other caligraphy in the plan. Quadrio refers to a
Tomaso Bezzi in a list that includes other great theatre architects, calling him 'lo stucchino'.
He had a great reputation throughout Italy and was born in Venice (Francesco Quadrio, *Della
Storia e della Razione d'Ogni Poesia*, 1744, vol. v, p. 544).
[4] Giovanni Bonlini, op. cit., p. 59.   [5] *Mercure Galant*, March 1683, pp. 250 et sqq.

autant de Figures humaines peintes en Marbre blanc, aussi en relief, et grandes comme le naturel, soutenant les Piliers qui en font la séparation. Ce sont des Hommes avec des Massues, des Esclaves, des Termes de l'un et de l'autre Sexe, et des Groupes de petits Enfans, le tout disposé de maniere que les plus pesantes et massives sont au dessous et les plus legeres au dessus.

Le haut, et le Plafonds de la Salle est peint d'une feinte Architecture en forme de Gallerie, à l'un des bouts de laquelle et du costé du Théatre, sont les Armes de Grimani, et au dessus une Gloire de quelque Divinité de la Fable, avec quantité de petits Enfans aislez qui accommodent des Guirlandes de Fleurs.

Le Théatre des Acteurs a treize toises et trois pieds de Longueur,[1] sur dix toises et deux pieds de Largeur,[2] estant élevé à proportion. Il est ouvert par un grand Portique de la hauteur de la Salle, dans l'épaisseur duquel sont encor quatre Palcs de chaque costé de la mesme simétrie que les autres, mais beaucoup plus ornez et enrichis; et dans la Voûte ou Arcade, deux Renommées avec leurs Trompetes paroissent suspendues en l'air, et une Vénus au milieu, qu'un petit Amour caresse.

Une heure avant l'ouverture du Théatre, le tableau de cette Vénus se retire, et donne jour à une grande ouverture, d'où descend une maniere de Lustre à quatre branches d'étofe d'or et d'argent, de douze à quatorze pieds de hauteur, dont le corps est un grand Cartouche des Armes de Messieurs Grimani, avec une Couronne de Fleurs-de-Lys, et de rayons surmontez de Perles au dessus. Le Chandelier porte quatre grands Flambeaux de poing de Cire blanche, qui éclairent la Salle, et demeurent allumez jusqu'à ce qu'on leve la Toile, et alors le tout s'évanouit, et revient à son premier état. Dés que la Piece est finie, cette Machine paroist de nouveau pour éclairer les Spectateurs, et leur donner lieu de sortir à leur aise, sans confusion.

By 1700, thirty-eight new operas had been put on here. It exists today as the Teatro Malibran.[3] Finally, a small theatre near the church of S. Giobbe was put up by Marco Morosini in 1679. But it closed in 1689 when the opera running, *Il Paolo Emilio* by P. R. Pignatta, was moved to the new theatre of San Fantino, a building that stood close to the present opera-house La Fenice, an eighteenth-century theatre. It was 'fort petit, mais bien peint' with three rows of boxes with twenty-three to each row.[4]

Of the other theatres put up for occasional performances in private houses there are a few further names; in the Canaregio there was a

---

[1] 82 ft. 7 in.   [2] 63 ft. 6 in.

[3] Antonio Groppo, *Notizia generale de' teatri della città di Venezia*, Venice, 1766, pp. 13–14, gives an interesting note of the existence of a puppet theatre, an exact replica of that in San Giovanni Grisostomo, put up in the Palazzo Labia by its owner Antonio Labia in the early eighteenth century, in which even the orchestra and the audience, with moving figures in the boxes were portrayed, whilst a company of musicians gave the opera and moved the figures from behind. Labia provided miniature copies of the libretto, which he presented to the real audience. This interesting relic has been destroyed, but the puppet figures can be seen in the Museum at the Ca' Rezzonico in Venice.   [4] *Mercure Galant*, March 1683, p. 243.

private theatre in the Palazzo Altieri; another was to be found on the Zattere towards the church of Ogni Santi, built for a performance in 1679, and a second little private theatre in the Salizzada of San Moisè gave at least one performance in 1700. A school production of an opera, *Il Finto Esau*, composed and written by two masters, was given in a theatre in the parish of Santa Marina, close to the more famous San Giovanni Grisostomo in 1698.

The chronicles leave us with an impressive list of the works performed in these theatres, the building of which alone testifies to the great importance attached to opera from its beginnings sixty years before in the city. And no true picture of life in the Republic, or in Italy and beyond the Alps, can be had without taking it into consideration. Croce, having studied operatic conditions in Naples, hints that the true greatness of seventeenth-century Italy lies in the crowd of artists who contributed to this flourishing theatrical life. He sees it not as the nadir of western civilization, but as a period of germination for all romantic thought. From the philological interests to the court poets, the scene-painters and architects, *maestri di cappella* singers and actors, the old Italy conferred her final benefits on European culture. 'Fu come un ultimo beneficio che la vecchia Italia rese alla cultura europea nei secoli nei quali si suole considerarla decadente o decaduta.'[1]

[1] Benedetto Croce, *Storia della Età Barocca in Italia*, Bari, 1929, p. 39.

The Spectacle

In many ways the spectacle presented on the stage of a Venetian opera-house was less remarkable in its novelty than the auditorium itself. The machinery was astonishingly ingenious and the sets most magnificent. But an audience in the mid-seventeenth century was accustomed to similar sights, not only in the theatre, but in other entertainments and ceremonials of court and civic life itself. The masques and pageants that were a characteristic of Elizabethan and Jacobean England are representative of a European tradition. In fact Inigo Jones was saturated with Italian stage practice as a glance at any of his designs will show.[1] A description of the epilogue to Thomas Carew's *Coelum Britannicum* (1634) might read as a passage from the diary of any seventeenth-century traveller who had attended *intermedii* in one of the Italian courts.

> For conclusion to this masque [writes Sir Henry Herbert], there appeares com-ming forth from one of the sides, as moving by a gentle wind, a great cloud, which arriving at the middle of the heaven, stayeth; this was of severall colours, and so great, that it covered the whole Scene. Out of the further part of the heaven beginnes to breake forth two other Clouds, differing in colour and shape; . . . the great Cloud beganne to breake open, out of which stroke beames of light; and in the midst suspended in the Ayre, sate Eternity on a Globe.

The description would fit many Italian Scenes. And indeed the designs for *Germanico sul Reno*[2] indicate the methods used in the celebrated cloud-machines of Venice. The decorated chariots filled with figures from classical mythology, which were often introduced on to the Venetian stage were familiar sights in all the festivities both popular and courtly of the high Renaissance. In fact, processions of decorated chariots in the streets of Florence, for example during carnival time, united both a traditional love of display with a conscious development of indigenous song uncommon in the fifteenth century when northern musicians predominated throughout Italy. Certainly an element of the

---

[1] *Designs by Inigo Jones for Masques and Plays at Court*, Walpole Society, vol. xii, Oxford, 1924.
[2] Plates 8–11.

canti carnascialeschi can be seen in many of the prologues and epilogues of early operas, not so much in the music, which does not often survive from the seventeenth century, but rather in the descriptions of the decorated chariots and the acting required for the symbolic poems which Ghisi mentions in his studies of the period[1] and which recall the later prologues and epilogues.

This love of display had had a long history and the means for obtaining it were fully understood by the Italians long before the invention of the basso continuo and recitative music upon which the *dramma per musica* or *favola in musica* are based. Since so much attention had been devoted to stage design in the previous century, the early operas were largely dependent upon it for success. And the traditional machines, therefore, played an important part in the layout of the new art. For the proportions of the visual and aural required in performance had yet to be determined.

In mid-seventeenth-century Venice for the first time it was possible, because of the great demand for works of this nature, to experiment and thus to discover the proportions of music, poetry, and design required in the new art. For the music, a study of the development of Cavalli's style is useful as showing the lines along which the search for the most reliable means of musical expression were sought. For the poem, the customs of both French and Spanish drama were drawn on to form a style of libretto which became international. The balance between music and drama, it is often said, was upset by Metastasio in the eighteenth century at the expense of the drama. But it is not sufficiently realized how precarious that balance had always been. The difficulties with which the early opera composers, librettists, and designers had to contend in order to give public satisfaction whilst preserving artistic merit have been overlooked. Monteverdi, Gluck, and Wagner have been linked together as the keystones of a three-arched bridge. Yet Monteverdi, although the composer of magnificent operas, is hardly concerned in the struggle to discover the perfect form for the medium. His scores of course show that he was perfectly clear as to the direction in which opera should go. But he wrote few works for the public theatre, and his death in 1643 deprived the operatic stage of its most clear-sighted advocate. Although Cavalli had assimilated his

[1] Federico Ghisi, *Feste Musicali della Firenza Medicea*, Florence, 1939, and *I canti carnascialeschi nelle fonti musicali del XV e XVI secolo*, Florence–Rome, 1937.

mentor's ideas on the subject and had written his *Didone* (1641) at the same time as the older master was himself engaged upon works for the public stage in Venice, there is little trace of Monteverdi's influence on the subsequent form of opera. Contemporaries considered him the foremost musician of the age. But there is little indication that later seventeenth-century composers had any first-hand knowledge of either *Il Ritorno d'Ulisse in Patria* or *L'incoronatione di Poppea*; the libretto of the former was never printed and the second only in a collection of Busenello's works *Ore ociose* in 1656; it was revived in Venice in 1646 and was given a performance in Naples in 1657: the libretto of his first opera for the public stage *L'Adone* (1639) fails to mention him as the composer and implies the authorship to Manelli.[1] And, in fact, his latest biographer is not entirely certain that the work is by Monteverdi.[2] Although the whole course of music itself after 1600 is dependent upon him, the delicate balances between the elements of opera-composition were only beginning to be appreciated at his death.

The art of libretto-writing was scarcely five years old. And its history deserves a chapter for itself. The most ancient of the three elements which combine to form opera was the visual. Great artists and architects had been employed in stage design. And it followed that the more ingenious the designer of the machines the more anxious were the audience to see as many examples of his skill as possible. In fact, the designers and machine-makers such as Torelli had reputations as high as the author or composer of the work. The preface to one of the earlier operas explicitly states that the Andromeda myth has been adapted 'by my pen to Dramatic shape in the briefest of short times as a vehicle for the beauty of the machines and theatrical apparatus'.[3] Only then is the composer mentioned. It is probable that the problem, as facing Monteverdi and Cavalli, consisted in finding a means whereby the *dramma in musica* could unfold itself in a logical pattern as a connected story and yet maintain the machinery after which the audience hankered. Busenello, the librettist for the early operas of both composers, offered them suitable poems, although only Metastasio solved the problem: and it is not possible here to attempt the much-needed reassessment of his place in the history of opera. But

---

[1] Alfred Loewenberg, op. cit., p. 10.   [2] Leo Schrade, op. cit., p. 347.
[3] *Il Bellero Fonte* [sic] *Drama Musicale Del Sig^r: Vincenzo Nolfi da f.* 1642 (from the author to the reader).

Metastasio is certainly a link in the connexion between Monteverdi
and Gluck, whereas the paths taken by French opera from Lully to
Rameau derive, although in a refined form, from the machine operas
in which opportunities for display supersede dramatic intensity. Supporters of 'les coins du roi et de la reine' are as active now as they were
in the eighteenth century, and it seems just as difficult to praise the
one without being considered to detract from the other as it was then;
it is unfortunate, since without Italian opera and the French opéra-
ballet the great works of Gluck are inconceivable; in fact the ballet
and the element of the supernatural come from France where they had
been traditional, even in the seventeenth century. Nevertheless, the
debt owed to Italy by Lully, not only from upbringing but from the
Italian company, including both Cavalli and the designer Torelli, who
visited Paris during his formative years, must not be overlooked. And
it is significant that it was Torelli's handiwork which gained the
approval of the French audience, rather than the music, in spite of the
changes Cavalli introduced to satisfy Parisian taste. Briefly, the case
seemed to present itself in which either the machine or the music must
predominate. The dance which served in France as a link between the
music and the display is more or less non-existent in Italy until a
French influence is felt in the late-seventeenth-century operas of
Venice, an influence that must be attributed largely to the number of
French travellers who visited the city. But, fundamentally the Venetian
and French forms have little in common. The Roman style of cantata-
opera, less concerned with drama, and much favoured by the Barberinis has a great affinity to the French type. Yet in the early years,
lines which seem to us so divergent, the Lullian opera with its chorus,
its ballets and inevitable *deus ex machina,* and the Cavalli works with
lengthy passages of dramatic recitative, punctuated by arias increasing
in length as the years go on, and with no chorus or dancing worthy
of the name, were not so entirely disparate. The very first operas
brought to Venice by the Roman company of Manelli and Ferrari,[1]
whose portrait we reproduce, bear a great resemblance to the later
French style: the great benefit bestowed upon us from Venice came
from the genius of Monteverdi, followed up by Cavalli, both of whom
saw opportunities in the new art to present dramatic and passionate
situations on the stage.

[1] Plate 7.

The struggle between the two conceptions is evident during roughly the first decade of opera in Venice. There are the works of Monteverdi and Cavalli, historical subjects in which a definite story is told, in which each episode is contingent upon another; and there are the works shown at the Teatro Novissimo, in which the plot is obscured by a mass of detail inserted to show off the skill of the engineer. Both *Andromeda* and *Bellerofonte*[1] show how loosely connected, what little human interest, and what little opportunity there was for the passionate music of Monteverdi in a series of tableaux which bear as little relation to the familiar story as does the modern pantomime to a fairy-tale from which it derives its title. The sets for *Il Bellerofonte* and *Venere Gelosa* add to the vivid descriptions. The scenarios for which the plates are taken were dedicated the one to the Grand Duke Ferdinand II of Tuscany and the other to Cardinal Antonio Barberini, still powerful in Rome on the eve of the death of his Uncle Urban VIII, two men capable by their position of spreading its fame far and wide.[2] And, in fact, these designs gave a European reputation to Torelli. In consequence, he went to Paris to organize the stage for *La Finta Pazza*[3] in the Salle du Petit Bourbon (14 December 1645), with which on 14 January 1641 the Teatro Novissimo had opened.

The number of changes of scenery introduced into some operas is mentioned by Badovero the librettist of Monteverdi's *Il Ritorno d'Ulisse in Patria*, in the preface to another of his plots on the same subject, *L'Ulisse errante*.[4] 'Daily', he says, 'there appears a greater number of scene-changes which were forbidden before.' Equally one of Cavalli's librettists, Bissari, remarks on the number of changes of scene introduced about this time. But significantly he draws a parallel between modern practice and its classical counterpart, quoting a sixteenth-century commentary of Vitruvius.[5] It seems strange that he should

---

[1] A translation of the scenario and the original designs for this opera together with the apparati scenici by Torelli forms Appendix V.

[2] *Apparati scenici per lo teatro Novissimo di Venetia*, 1644.

[3] Henry Prunières, *L'Opéra italien en France avant Lulli*, Paris, 1913. This book shows the interest taken by Mazarin and the trouble he was prepared to spend scouring the Italian courts for singers and designers for the opera.

[4] *L'Ulisse errante*, Opera musicale, Venice, 1644. Text, Badovero; music, Sacrati (SS. Gio. e P.): 'e al presente per dare soddisfattione all' occhio, pare precetti ciò che all' hora era prohibito, inventandosi ogni giorno maggior numero di cambiamenti di Scene.'

[5] *La Torilda*. Dramma per i moderni Teatri. Venice, 1648. Text, Bissari; music, Cavalli (T. San Cass.): 'Trà le più osservate curiosità de' moderni Drammi, habbiamo la varietà delle Scene, che tratte in giro, ò condotte per canaletti di legno con machina, ch'ad in un subito le

consider it necessary to seek classical precedent when the very fact that he uses a modern commentary would indicate that such practices had been known, at any rate, for a century.

It was the popularity of this type of production that set the artistic problem for Cavalli to solve. A libretto packed with incidents suitable for the large-scale use of machines was not sufficiently dramatic to warrant constant repetition without the danger of boring the public. The historical and romantic plots dealt with human affairs and would appeal to an Italian audience if a means could be found to introduce machines consistent with the ultimate aim, to move the affections, to employ contemporary phraseology. Therefore the machines had to be adapted so that it was possible to incorporate them into the human story, and extend to everyday affairs that which had been associated with the *deus ex machina*; if necessary the most elaborate and cumbersome machines, which could only be introduced for their own sakes, were treated, as in the old *intermedii*, as prologue or epilogue. But, in general, the machines were carefully worked into the plot—rising moon or moving corpse, crashing masonry or burning castle.

The type of machine required is occasionally given below the list of *dramatis personae* in the librettos. *Scipione Africano*[1] is an example:

> Discesa di Siface da una Torre.
> Trasporto della Sibilla per aria de' Spiriti.
> Apparsa dell' Iride.
> Volo d'un Aquila intorno la Scena.
> Sparimento della Sibilla.
> Precipicio d'uno senza offendersi.

Here Cavalli seems to have solved the problem and is able to introduce machines without interrupting the story; *Scipione Africano* was written after his return from Paris and it is possible that he was influenced by French taste to include a number of machines into the

recambia, vanno per ogni parte aprendo nuovi prospetti: ma se ciò si chiederà dell' antichi non mancherà chi risponda "Scena, aut versatilis cum machinis subito vertebatur, aut ductilis cum tractis tabulatis hac atque illac interioris pictura nudabatur".' The commentary on Vitruvius reads 'Ea aut versilis fuit, quum subito tota machinis quibusdam verteretur, et aliam picturae faciem ostenderet, aut ductilis quum tractis tabulatis hac atque illac species picturae nuderetur interior.' Gulielmi Philandri Castilionii Galli civis RO. In Decem libros M. Vitruvii Pollionis de Architectura Annotationes, Rome, 1544, p. 162.

[1] *Scipione Africano*. Drama per musica nel Teatro à SS. Gio. e Paolo, Venice, 1664. Text, Minato; music, Cavalli. This libretto was translated as *Der Grossmüthige Scipio* and set by Krieger in Weissenfels in 1690 (Loewenberg, p. 45).

body of the drama, realizing the importance to his own dramatic aims of proving to an Italian audience that it was possible to combine the passionate elements of his own style with a desire for scenic thrills on the part of the audience. But in spite of Cavalli's attempts, for the moment the machine-opera was to gain in popularity. However, the real nature of opera had been made clear for subsequent musicians such as Scarlatti to develop. But, until the end of the century, there are large additions to the stage requirements. Nineteen years later, in *Giustino*,[1] the machines required both within the action and for the final 'gloria' or epilogue reached outstanding numbers.

> Act I. Aratro tirato da Bovi che si spezza.
> La Fortuna sopra la ruota, che gira.
> Mostro Selvaggio che vien sbranato.
> Elefante carico di Genti da Guerra.
> Carro dell' Allegrezza che guida il Ballo.

> Act II. Mare tempestoso con Armata Navale che scorre naufragio.
> Nave reale che combattuta dell' onde si rompe ad un scoglio.
> Dragone Marina ch'esce dal Mare, e combatte.
> Torre dalla sommita della quale precipitano due prigioneri.
> Carro falcato tirato da Cavalli carico di Guerrieri, che si travolge.

> Act III. Ombra ch'esce da'un sepolcro.
> Il Tempio dell' Eternità, con la Gloria.

All the technical details required for such instructions could have been found in Sabbattini's book. No doubt his methods had been perfected, but there had been no call for new technique. It is interesting to see how the distinction between the sets for the action and the machines for *intermedii*, as he saw them and distinguished them in his two books, has disappeared. But the excesses of later operas such as *Giustino* certainly detracted from the artistic value, turning it into a purely sensational entertainment that caused its disrepute in intellectual society until Apostolo Zeno made an attempt to bring back the librettos to a more simple pattern.

However, although there is no doubt that the machines were given undue preponderance late in the century, there is a danger that their part in the action will be underestimated and that they will be considered solely as a method of appealing to the seventeenth-century love of display. This would be a wrong conclusion, leaving out of

---

[1] *Giustino*. Melodrama da rappresentarsi nel celebre Teatro Vendramino di San Salvatore, Venice, 1683. Text, Berengan; music, Legrenzi.

account the intellectual content, deriving from a use of symbolism which gave a universal application to these contrivances and helped to explain the plot as a means to ultimate edification. For example, the cast in *Penelope la casta*[1] includes, apart from the principals, a lengthy list of abstract figures such as 'necesità del governo' and 'politica di Stato'. And the moral purpose of the plot is made clear in a prologue in which appear 'Il possibile, e l'impossibile, il Dubio, e Temerità amorosa sopra un carro tirato dalle Colombe di Venere'. Almost certainly the audience would have been able to recognize each figure from the conventional clothes or ornaments which were carried. And the symbolical arrangements of the figures were easily interpreted through such conventions. The symbolism continues in the prologue with the appearance of 'una nave a piene vele col Merito a prova la Costanza, il Valor, e la Gloria'. Later these figures are supported by Truth and the directions read 'vola la Temerità, e all' apparer della Verità precipita abagliata' [*sic*]. Of particular interest in this opera is the link between the symbolical machine and the music, for at the end of the second act we are presented with 'Immensa frà l'aria, e la terra'. Seated in this great void is Imaginatione who is seen thinking, during which time the character of her thoughts is shown in the music. We read of a 'Sonata, che dinota pensier allegro' which Imaginatione considers 'troppo allegro'; the music alters and now it is 'troppo mesto'; 'da caccia' is played and the figure says 'non vò caccia'; 'bisbetico' (whimsical), 'ne men questo', she says; 'Danze'; the music plays, 'eh danza non voglio', we are told; 'profondo', the music continues and is stopped with the comment 'pensier d'Erebo và sottera'; at last the music is savage, 'fiero', and Imaginatione cries 'sì, sì, guerra, venga guerra'. And the whole scene changes as War enters with 'Insoferenza su Carro di Foca'. The absence of illustrations makes it impossible to say exactly how all such figures were clothed. But it is certain that there were garments conventionally used for such figures, similar to the directions given by Sabbattini for making the machine for Iris or the Rainbow.[2] In the elaborate production of *Ercole in Tebe* in Florence, Iris rides on a rainbow and Juno never appears without her peacocks; equally, in the sets for *Giustino*, Fortuna appears on her revolving wheel. Each

---

[1] *Penelope la casta.* Drama per musica da rappresentarsi nel Famosissimo Teatro Grimano in S. Gio. Grisostomo, Venice, 1685. Text, Noris; music, Pallavicino.

[2] Niccolò Sabbattini, op. cit., p. 136 (ed. 1942).

character had certain conventional attributes which added point to his appearance. Such detail concerned the minor characters and machines as well. In *Marcello in Siracusa*[1] the frontispiece is an emblem of the story showing Archimedes with a mirror (plate 6a). And the finale of Act I consists of 'gli scolari d'Archimede, con istromenti Geometrici' who form 'una capriciosa danza'. The whole opera is an example of the wealth of scenery needed to satisfy the late-seventeenth-century audience.

Act I. 1. Riviera del Porto di Siracusa con tre Rocche. Nel mare lontano armata navale di Marcello. Sù la cima d'ultima Roccha Archimede con il concavo vetro; nel Cielo il Sole, sù la Riviera Ierone Rè, e sopra Trono emminente con popolo spettatore alla machina . . . qui un raggio del Sole vibrato dal vetro di Archimede và serpando nelle navi Romane.

5. Reggia di Siracusa.

9. Campo d'armi, dove stà attendato l'esercito Romano, per espugnatione di Siracusa.

10. Giardino reale irrigato da un ramo del Fiume Imera.

21. Archimede da due suoi scolari fattosi recare la famosa sfera di vetra in cui vedavansi girar gl'Orbi stellati, sede sotto un arco di Lauri.

24. Gli scolari d'Archimede, con istromenti Geometrici formano capricciosa danza.

Act II. 1. Solitudine delitiosa con acque, e fontane.

7. Boschetto di delitie trà i recinti della Reggia, bagnato dal fonte d'Aretusa riserbata per la Caccia de volatili.

16. Sala reale.

28. Loco disabitato con Antro à piè d'uno Tor. Notte. Ballo di prigioni usciti alla libertà.

Act III. 1. Loggie Reali.

6. Stanze nel Palaggio di Ierone.

17. Campo de Romani col soccorso venuto da Roma.

19. Appartamento d'Archimede con istromenti geometrici.

Sometimes the symbolism is geographical. *La Doriclea*[2] is an elaborate and surprisingly early example of a libretto with a consecutive story yet with many scene-changes. But it is noticeable that the interest is concentrated on symbolism in the sets and little attention is paid to machines. There was as yet no merging of the two.

Prologo. Il monte della Virtù, nelle cui cime si rimira il tempio della gloria.

---

[1] *Marcello in Siracusa*. Drama per musica nel famoso Teatro Grimano (SS. G. e P.), Venice, 1670. Text, Noris; music, Boretti.

[2] *La Doriclea*. Dramma musicale rappresentata nel teatro di S. Cassiano in Venetia, 1645. Text, Faustini; music, Cavalli.

Act I. 1. Si figura la Scena alpestre, e sassoso, divisa dall' Arasse, fiume che nato nel Monte Tauro scorre per lunghissimi tratti per Oriente fino nella Media Atropaia, hora detta Servan, indi rivolgendosi pe [*sic*] l'aspetto Settentrionale verso Occidente, e congiuntosi con il Ciro, dopo haver irrigate le Campagne d'Artassata Città dell' Arminia, e la pianura Arassena sbocca nel mare Caspio.

Act II. 1. Città d'Artassata.
   2. Deserto tra l'Arminia, e l'Assiria.
   5. Cortile del Palagio supremo d'Artassata, alloggiamento d'Artabane.
  10. Reggia di Marte.

Act III. 1. Giardino.
   4. Altro Cortile del Palagio supremo d'Artassata.
  10. Stanze Reali.
  17. Appartamenti d'Artabano.
  21. (*Last scene*) Varie perspettivi di Villaggi, e di Città di Armene.

The scene for the first act is very typical of the mind of the age: a journey through different perspectives suggestive of the wandering of the passions. It is a conceit symbolizing the complicated love interest seen on the stage. The passions as rivers flow through the various situations until joining at last they disburse their waters into a sea of love. In fact the scene has a geographical foundation, there being a river Arax that is joined by the Kur in Georgia, having its mouth in the middle of the western shore of the Caspian sea. Bisaccioni[1] explains many of Torelli's celebrated *Apparati Scenici*, the designs for which are included here with those for *Il Bellerofonte*, as symbols representative of human nature. Plate 19*a* represents the island of Nasso with its city shown in the far distance. This, he considers, demonstrates the workings of the mind, for 'the things farthest away and most difficult to

[1] Conte Maiolino Bisaccioni, *Apparati Scenici Per lo Teatro Novissimo di Venetia Nell' anno 1644 d'inventione e cura di Iacomo Torelli da Fano*, Venice, 1644: 'Viddesi al rimuovere della Cortina una delitiosa boscareccia, che rappresentava l'Isola di Nasso, la cui Città appariva in un prospetto lontanissimo, e qui ben l'occhio diede à divedere all' anima, che le cose più lontane, e difficili da ottenersi, e più care, e più desiderate ne sono, poichè sprezzato per così dire, il verde della campagna, che pure suol essere il ristoro, e la delitia d'una vista, corse veloce per quegli ampii viali à considerare la Città, che non dipinta, ma di rilievo sembrava, tanto ben era, stò per direi organizzata della pittura, e animata da' lumi, che sapevano far spiccare dall'ombre adattate, e le case, e le torri, e le mura distinte. Goduto questo estremo della vista, si rivolsero gl'occhi non ben satii ancora al rimanente della Scena; era questi un' ordine fregolato di trè grandi viali: distinti dalli arbori, quasi da pareti, che andavano à terminare in una vasta campagna, nel cui mezzo, come dissi, era la Città. Ardirei di dire, che questa Scena fosse un simbolo dalla vita nostra, poichè la gioventù guidata perli trè vie, del piacere, del sapere, e dell' utile, si conduce all' ampiezza della virilità, che termina poi nella nassa della morte, o d'una tomba, e guida alla Cittadinanza del Cielo, ultimo punto della prospettiva dell' huomo.'

PLATE 6

a. Marcello in Siracusa
(Frontispiece from the libretto Venice, 1670)

b. Eteocle e Polinice
(Frontispiece from the libretto Venice, 1675)

obtain are the dearest and most desired. The green of the country, as you might say, that should be the comfort and delight of a view, is spurned and the eye runs away quickly through the spacious avenues to consider the city.' After he has described how the city is contrived, not by painting but in relief brought out by ingenious lighting, he brings the audience back to consider the foreground, the scene cut by the three great avenues of trees almost like walls that lead up into a spacious countryside with the city in the centre. 'I would dare to say', he continues, 'that this scene may be a symbol of our life. Youth is led through the three roads, pleasure, knowledge and gain, reaches the fullness of manhood, and finally ends in the net of death and the tomb leading to the citizenship of heaven, the ultimate point in the perspective of man.'

Machines, too, should be studied as images; and in many cases they become more than a distraction or an appeal to the baser taste for display, although of course such an element plays a large part. They have changed from the ancient *deus ex machina* which appeared as the providential solution to a human entanglement, favoured in France, and have become figures with a more universal mission. It must be remembered also that machines which to our eyes appear of great splendour were in the seventeenth century a commonplace. Juno without her peacocks and Iris without a rainbow might have been a distraction, but treated in the conventional way they were an aid to the better understanding of the plot.

Nevertheless, although a love of symbolism may explain a number of machines, it does not justify an excessive use of them at the expense of the music. The whole purpose of opera is destroyed when the purely visual is allowed to supersede the music, as in *Galieno*,[1] which opens 'senza il solito concerto degl' Istromenti apparisce Vasta pianura sotto Celo di oscura Notte'. To the right of the stage a great car is gradually illuminated by the rising sun. And in it Idea, crowned and with wings, is seated above celestial globes, at her feet are the kingdoms and empires of the world, and she is surrounded by her children, 'varii, e d'elevati pensieri'. From the top of the stage an imperial audience-chamber lit with candles slowly descends. In it are seated Galieno and Fulvia with the ladies and gentlemen of the court around them, and

---

[1] *Galieno.* Drama da rappresentarsi nel Famosissimo Teatro Grimano di SS. Giò. e Paolo, Venice, 1676. Text, Noris; music, Pallavicino.

instruments for the dance. Here is an example of an opera in which music is neglected. The work of the overture is taken over by the machine. That is an extreme case. But there are many instances of a trumpet call followed by a splendid procession serving in the place of an overture. *Ariberto e Flavio*[1] opens with a view of a bastion which inexplicably crashes to the ground; when 'al un tocca semplice di Trombe rinversa parte del Baloardo, con lo scapio d'una Mina'. The noise must have startled the audience into silence if they could not be induced to pay attention to the music.

There is very little first-hand evidence of the means whereby these machines were worked in the actual theatres. One primary source is a collection of drawings for the Teatro San Salvatore, now in the library of the Opéra in Paris. They are designs for *Germanico sul Reno*[2] by Legrenzi, one of the more important Venetian composers. His operas are always written on the grand scale, for which this theatre seems to have been well adapted. For example, the double stage required in *Eteocle e Polinice* is shown as plate 6*b*.

The particular interest of the designs lies in the comparison offered between the fully decorated set and the bare mechanism, the pulleys and levers by which the apotheosis is contrived or the cloud opened as illustrated in Plates 8–11. The mechanism in Plate 8 is a simple arrangement of pulleys dependent upon a winch situated in the roof, which enabled the wooden frame to be lowered on to the stage with the characters already seated in the places provided. It was in effect a *tableau vivant*. The machine is made so that the various parts can work independently, and the side-platforms would enable a number of *comparse* or 'supers' to climb on to it. In Plate 8 it appears to be fully drawn up into the roof. The decorations would be attached to the framework, some of the clouds being painted or fixed to the oblong flats outlined in the illustration. The movable struts attached to the ropes allow for a measure of play in the clouds and may help to support certain of the characters, such as the three women on the right in Plate 9, who are attached to no definite row of seats. The circular frame with the appearance of an astrolabe on the left must move independently. For this machine must be the means by which the man

[1] *Ariberto e Flavio*, regi de' Longobardi, drama per musica da rappresentarsi nel restaurato famoso Teatro Vendramino di San Salvatore, Venice, 1684. Text, Cialli; music, Lonati.

[2] *Germanico sul Reno*. Drama per musica da rappresentarsi nel famosissimo Teatro Vendramino di San Salvatore, Venice, 1676. Text, Corradi; music, Legrenzi.

PLATE 7

BENEDETTO FERRARI

(from the libretto of *La Maga Fulminata*. Venice, 1638, p. 28)

PLATE 8

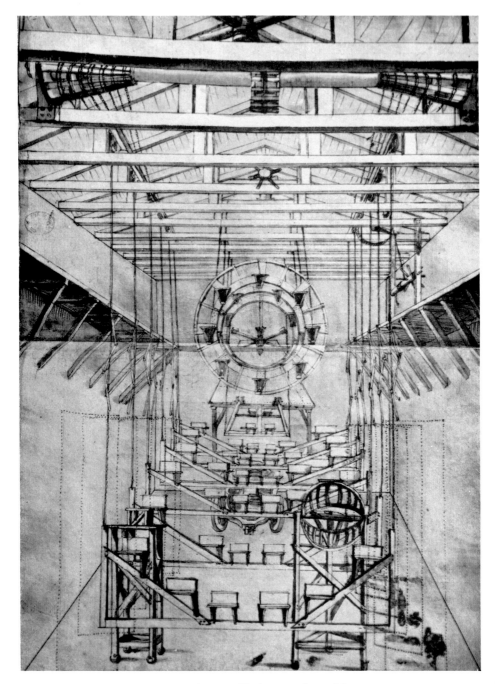

Germanico sul Reno. Undecorated machinery

PLATE 9

Germanico sul Reno. Decorated machinery

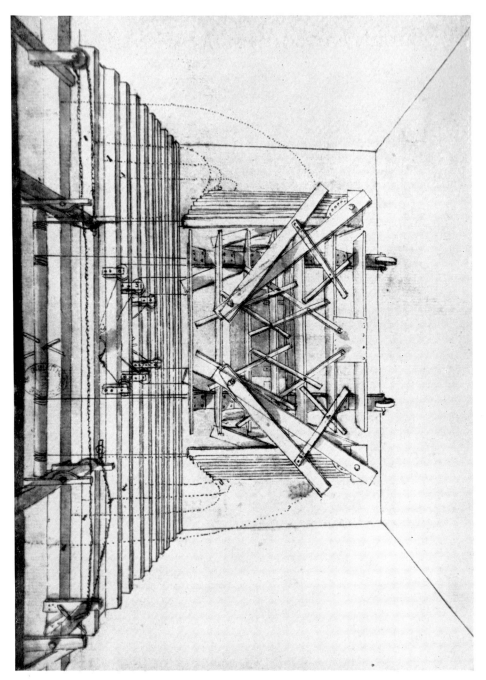

Germanico sul Reno. Descending cloud machinery

PLATE II

a. Descending cloud closed

b. Descending cloud open

Germanico sul Reno

in Plate 9 appears to be flung to the ground. What appears to be some wrathful god is seated firmly within the astrolabe, which is covered to look like a shell, whilst the subject of the manœuvre is bound to his seat, that can be seen as the flat piece of wood on top of the astrolabe in Plate 8. When this revolves, it appears as if he were being hurled to the ground. Plates 10 and 11 illustrate a similar if less elaborate scene in which a cloud opens to disclose the prospect of a *gloria*, the 'glory' in Jacobean descriptions. In Plate 10 we can see that the machine is lowered at the back of the stage. Plate 11*a* shows the mechanism shut with clouds drawn across the scene. It remains closed through the weight of the main struts as shown in Plate 10. But when the ropes are pulled taut the struts, on the lever system, expand to disclose the triumphal tableau of Plate 11*b*. The transverse rope enables the whole machine to move across the stage. But there must be some hidden cog that enables it to move forward on the two wheels at the base. If this theatre was built on a similar plan to SS. Giovanni e Paolo, there would be sufficient room for it to be held in front of the larger and more static machine; for according to the plan that theatre had four sets of perspective shutters. The elaborate type was evidently in general use since other pictures show similar machines. The effect could be guaranteed to impress: it had been used with success by Inigo Jones in Jacobean masques and still delighted the audience in 1695. Arteaga[1] describes the wonders of such a piece in *Pastor d'Anfriso* given in San Giovanni Grisostomo, in which the Palace of the Sun, all of glass, and glinting with different colours, is let down from the roof. There is an interesting plan and illustration giving the final effect of a machine in *La Costanza e Fortezza* (1723)[2] by Fux, performed in Prague, which shows a 'glory', giving a choice of four possible sets. This series of machines, three in all, for the final machine is a variation of the first, appears to work on a different plan to those in Venice, and it is difficult to decide whether it descends from the roof or not, since the details are not given. Certainly the layout of the stage is less modern although considerably later than that given in the plan of SS. Giovanni e Paolo; the wings are parallel to the front of the stage and show no attempt to employ the latest perspective effects, nor have the machines the com-

[1] Stefano Arteaga, op. cit., vol. i, p. 327: 'Si vide scendere dell' alto il palazzo del Sole di vaghissima e bellissima architectura lavorato di dentro e di fuori con cristalli a diversi colori, i quali con singolare maestria si volgevano in giro continualmente.'
[2] *D.T.O.*, vol. xvii, ed. E. Wellesz, 1910.

pactness of those in Venice. But, since the plan is less detailed, we cannot give any exact description of the method of manipulation. The efficiency and ease with which the Venetians ran their opera-houses was, in a sense, the cause of the decline in musical standards during the last twenty years of the century. For, instead of using technical proficiency to aid the real functions of opera, the music was treated as the servant, forced in extreme cases to relinquish its position entirely. Cavalli, it could be said, had been too thorough in his self-appointed task. He had proved that display could heighten the effect of music in the new *dramma per musica*: his successors had carried his ideas to the absurd length of using machines as the principal means of gaining the effects which, in opera, should be obtained by the music.

The Aria

Although the arias become so much the best-known parts of an Italian
opera they were, in fact, the final contribution to operatic form in
Venice. Originally they were additions to the *favola in musica* inserted
to attract a larger audience; their purpose can be identified in some
measure with that of the machines, relics of the *intermedii* that delighted
renaissance audiences as entr'actes in performances of plays. For this
reason it is important to interpret the title *favola in musica* in a strict
sense. It is a story told musically by means of the new declamatory
style of singing. The story was rendered more expressive through the
power of the recitative alone. And unlike the later development of
opera structure the ariette, for aria is too inflated a term, were not
strictly part of the drama but were interpolated. In the early part of
the period in Venice, the means whereby a composer intensified the
more dramatic moments was achieved by an alteration of the recitative into a more lyrical and flowing melody, or by the addition of an
orchestral accompaniment to this arioso if an even greater effect was
desired. In the second edition of *Il Bellerofonte* (1645) three little
strophic songs conclude the libretto. They are marked 'canzonette
aggiunte all' opera'. And, although they bear textual relation to the
previous scene, they were certainly intended more as lyrical interludes
than as extensions of the plot. They seem to resemble the canzonas
of the Florentine carnival of the previous century, the four-part
songs in which the upper voice dominates the rest in an early
attempt at monody.[1] They may derive from the villanellas of sixteenth-century composers, such men as Marenzio who wrote songs
'all so conceived that they can be sung as monodies to a bass'. In this,
Einstein continues, 'they become a model for all such products at the
end of the century'.[2] In fact the collections of solo songs published
in the early part of the seventeenth century have much in common
with the later arias. For instance, a comparison of an aria from

[1] Federico Ghisi, *Feste Musicali della Firenze Medicea*, Florence, 1939, pp. 29 sqq.
[2] Alfred Finstein, *The Italian Madrigal*, p. 587.

L'Orontea (1666) with a poem set by Sigismondo d'India, an 'aria di guerra amorosa' will show how close was the link in the literary style.

Donzelletta	Voi vaccatrici
Vezzosetta	Saettatrici
D'ascoltarti non mi pento	Pungenti rose
Con gl'accenti	Trombe amorose
Tuoi pungenti	O bocche innamorate
Scherza pur ch'io son contento[1]	Mordete, sfidate, ferite, piagate.[2]

They were simple little songs. And the example from Boretti's *Claudio Cesare*[3] (1672) may well be compared to the villanella Einstein quotes,

Boretti, Claudio Cesare. Act II. 15 (1672)

in which 'an exuberant operatic Cupid makes his entrance',[4] although the subject-matter here is different. But the extreme brevity and slight musical character of this little song mark it off from the set aria whether fully developed in the da capo style or a lengthy strophic song and link it with the older collection of pieces. Even the texts for the chorus, scarcely used in later operas but still to be found in early works of Cavalli, seem to show a connexion with the older villanella. The

---

[1] *L'Orontea.* Drama per musica di D. Hiacinto Andrea Cicognini da rappresentarsi nel Teatro Grimano di SS. Giò e Paolo. Venice, 1666. Act I. 11; music, Cesti. The prologue to this opera is the same as that in *La Doriclea* (1645) by Faustini with music by Cavalli.

[2] *Classici italiani*, ed. Balsamo-Crivelli, vol. li, p. lxii.

[3] Act II. 15.   [4] Alfred Einstein, op. cit., pp. 588–9.

final line from a sextet[1] in *Le Nozze di Teti e di Peleo* is very similar to
that in the 'aria di guerra amorosa'.

> Volo precipite
> All sommo culmine
> O dio fedel
> Sprezza col fulmine
> L'angel bricipite
> Del dio crudel
> Battasi, vincasi, spegnasi il ciel.

Further confirmation for the suggestion that the aria began in Venice
by being considered independent of the main business of the drama
can be found from a study of the librettos themselves. There are many
indications that the songs were altered sometimes even for each evening. In *La Doriclea*,[2] an opera written before the tyranny of the singer
can be said to exist, so that the alterations cannot be ascribed to vanity
on their part, there are several little stanzas printed at the end for
insertion into the opera 'per dilettari gl'uditori e per aggradire à rap-
presentanti'. And eleven years later, in *Artemisia*,[3] a note after one song
announces that 'quest' aria ogni sera sarà variata'. But we must make
a distinction between these additions to the operas which denote a
link with the past, which fulfil a need as the older canzone had done,
and the craze for arias which superseded it; this craze may be ascribed
to the growing powers of the musician and singer and owes its popularity to the increased appreciation of the aesthetic value of the aria
when it is incorporated into the body of the score, 'come germogli
dalle radice'.[4] A poet of the old style of libretto-writing is Giovanni
Francesco Busenello whose methods can be studied from *L'incoronatione di Poppea*. Goldschmidt has printed the text separately in his
edition of the score.[5] A comparison of this text with one by Metastasio,
the master of eighteenth-century construction, will show the change
in style; Metastasio builds up his scene in the manner of a painting in
perspective in which the eye is directed along the line of sight to a
point beyond which the imagination must take charge, the recitative

---

[1] Act I. 1. Music example no. 9.
[2] *La Doriclea.* Dramma musicale rappresentata nel Teatro di S. Cassiano, Venice, 1645.
Text, Gio. Faustini: music, Cavalli.
[3] *Artemisia.* Drama per Musica nel Teatro a SS. Giò e Paolo. Venice, 1656. Text, N. Minato;
music, Cavalli. Act III. 9.
[4] Francesco Quadrio, *Della storia e della ragione d'ogni poesia*, Bologna, 1739–49, vol. v, p. 446.
[5] Hugo Goldschmidt, *Studien zur Geschichte der italienischen Oper im 17. Jahrhundert*, Leipzig, 1904.

EXAMPLE 1. Cavalli–Busenello, *La Didone* (1641). Act II. 2

is, for him, the line of direction beyond which the aria provides scope for the composer's fantasy. Subsequent developments of the powers of the orchestra reduced the need for his distinctions between fact, as it were, and fiction which greatly increased the range of the accompanied recitative, besides opening new fields of instrumental expression by the associations of tone colours and preparing the ground for a closer connexion between recitative and aria. The librettos of Boito, particularly his adaptations of Shakespeare, are a return to the older methods of Busenello in which lyrical phrases mingle with the strict recitative. An example of this style can be seen in *La Didone* (1641) set by Cavalli.[1] After Dido has spurned the love of Iarba he breaks into a lament:

> Disamato, disprezzato[2]
> Volgo il piè, ma non il core,
> Che schernito e mal gradito
> Tanto è fuori di se stesso,
> Quanto è dentro al suo dolore.

[1] Act II. 2. Music example No. 1.
[2] Unloved, despised, I turn away, but my heart remains, scorned, unwanted. Grief puts me

Crudele, empia, superba,
Bestemmiar, maledir(ti) il cor desia,
Ma al mio dispetto sei la vita mia.
Rivolgo altrove il piede,
El cor mio resta quì.
D'aita, e di mercede
Veder non spero il dì,
Insanabile mal m'opprime il core,
Son disperato, e pur nutrisco amore.
Derelitto, ramingo,
Didone, ahi dove andrò
Lagrimoso, e solingo
Le selci ammolirò;
Dirà (pur) sempre agonizando il core
Son disperato, e pur nutrisco amore.

It is apparent at once that the recitative and aria are not distinct as far as content is concerned. The aria quatrains differ in metre. But the punctuation ensures that no break occurs between them. Cavalli emphasizes the musical change by the term aria and insertion of the little ritornello. Yet the brevity of each verse and the absence of thematic connexion would justify the use of the term arioso to describe the lyrical passages had he not been so strict with his own term. But it is scarcely possible to see in this piece the germs of the great arias. The conception is different: here there is a desire to break up the strict recitative and the monotony of the poetic rhythms to render the passage more poignant. It is, in fact, following the traditions of Monteverdi in which music must be subordinate to text. The setting is straightforward with no reduplication of text such as might give scope to the formal genius of the composer. However, if we turn to a libretto of the last decade of the century, *Il furio Camillo* (1693) by M. Noris, who became court poet at Venice before Zeno but who was by birth a Venetian nobleman, we can see at once, both by the position of the verses at the end of the scene, and from the formal arrangement of the lines which allows for a flexible handling from the composer, that the music had become of paramount importance over the dramatic

out of my mind yet equally I am filled by it. My heart longs to curse and besmirch you, cruel, unholy and proud. Yet in spite of it you are my life. My steps turn elsewhere but my heart stays here. I hope never to see the day of recompense and help. I despair yet live in hopes of love. Deserted and a wanderer weeping and alone, ah, Dido, my tears shall soften the flint stones. Yet still, whatever I suffer, however I despair, I shall hope for love.

unity of the opera. The situation closely resembles that from *La Didone*, yet Noris's text lacks the passion of the earlier verses. He is content to leave that to the genius of the composer.

ATTO TERZO. SCENA V

Gilbo, Arideo pensoso

Signore? al fin t'indusse[1]
Lidia, donna sagace,
A procurar dolc' esca a la sua face.

Ar.　Ero de le mie doglie
Lo artefice Perillo:
Novo Bombice ignaro.

Gi.　(Quanto fia scaltra or la bellezza imparo.)

Ar.　Cerco aita all' altrui foco,
E hò quel foco anch' io nel cor.
E per doppia tirannia
Vò a tradir la fiamma mia
Per dar esca ad altro ardor.
Cerco, etc.

The aria assumed an importance deriving from its emotional powers. Its effect was compared to the 'sort of purging, and some release of emotion accompanied by pleasure'[2] of which Aristotle speaks in his description of 'melodies which competitors in musical contests ought to be required to use'. He is referring to an effective style suitable for expressing 'pity, and fear and inspiration' which, drawn up to a great tension, finds release in an outburst of sound. Hence in the seventeenth century the aria was placed at the end of a scene. The recitative had built up tension which was released by the formal song into which the composer, aided by the rhetorical art of the singer, poured the streams of his melodic invention. The poem was repeated in many different guises as the music interpreted each facet of the emotional situation for 'in these seasons of pain, or felicity, the heart changes every moment'.[3] It is unfortunate that Marcello has been taken so literally

---

[1] *Gilbo.* 'My Lord, in the end the wise Lidia compels you to discover sweet bait in her eyes.'
　　Arideo. 'I was for my pains the cunning Perillo; I do not know a new "Bombice".'
　　Gilbo. ('What cunning is needed now to gain beauty.')
　　Arideo. 'I seek aid from another fire. Yet I have fire even of my own. And for a double tyranny I want to betray my own flame to give food to another desire.'

[2] Aristotle, *Politics*, 1342a, tr. Barker.

[3] L. A. C. Bombet (Stendhal), *The Lives of Haydn and Mozart with observations on Metastasio*, 2nd ed., London, 1818, p. 433.

by students of eighteenth-century music. His satire *Teatro alla moda* explains the position of the aria purely on utilitarian grounds: the singer gains greater applause if he is able to leave the stage after a magnificent song. There is no doubt that he may. But a satire naturally concentrates on abuses of a custom which had primarily great aesthetic significance. The singer, by the nature of aria, had to leave the stage once his personal reactions to the situation had found relief. For the aria was the 'conclusion, the epilogue or epiphonema of the passion,' an escape, as Arteaga the celebrated critic put it, for the emotions.[1]

The arias fall into two distinct types. First, strophic songs with a definite rhyming and metrical scheme to which the music fits each of the varied number of stanzas, and secondly the da capo form in which the music and text, or the music alone of the first section returns to complete the form in an ABA structure. The repeat became ultimately the means whereby the singer could extemporize in numerous complicated divisions. In the original form, however, the first line or couplet were repeated to complete the songs. The Laments, which make an important body of arias, since they contain some of the most expressive music of the period, can be in either form, the characteristic feature being the various ground basses upon which they are built. Both types can be seen in two early operas by Cavalli. The strophic aria from *Gli Amori d'Apollo e di Dafne*[2] (1640) is a song with three verses connected by an instrumental ritornello. It occurs in the middle of a scene, for the position of the aria as a part of an aesthetic plan was not as yet thought of. However, this song is, in a way, an interpolation into the opera; Aurora is not one of the protagonists and the song bears little relation to the event enacted in the scene. The fact that it is marked 'aria' in the score tends to set it apart, too, from the regular action. The da capo example from *La Virtù degli strali d'amore*[3] (1642) is more the parent of the great eighteenth-century aria. Yet here it opens the scene. But, unlike the strophic song, it is not entitled 'aria' in the score. Yet the return to the recitative after the final cadence

---

[1] Stefano Arteaga, op. cit., vol. i, p. 28. 'Cotal situazione è la propria dell' *aria*, la quale considerata sotto questo filosofico aspetto non è altro che la conchiusione, l'epilogo o epifonema della passione, e il compimento più perfetto della melodia' or again 'se il personaggio non si risolve, ma rimane nelle sue dubbiezze, come tal volta addiviene, allora l'aria dovrà essere come un escita, una scappata del sentimento, cioè, quella riflessione ultima, in cui l'anima si trattiene per isfogar in quel momento il suo dolore o qualsivoglia altra affezione.'

[2] Act I. 1. Music example No. 2.

[3] Act II. 4. Music example No. 3.

EXAMPLE 2. Cavalli–Busenello, *L'Amori d'Apollo e di Dafne* (1640). Act I. 1

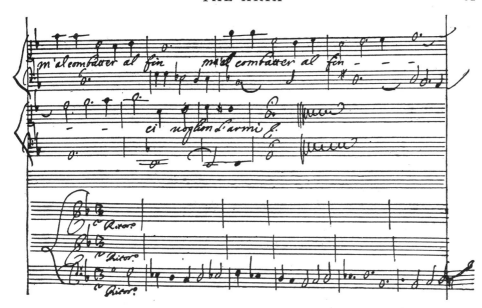

leaves us in no doubt that the composer intended that it should be
considered as a formal song. In this example the voice is given no
divisions in the repeat section. The orchestral response to the vocal
phrases brings to mind the early concerto style. There is, too, a tendency to prolong the vocal line in the middle section. In the light of
subsequent developments it is curious that the middle section should
be more elaborate and the da capo a simplification rather than an
elaboration of the first statement. The first part of this aria reaches
to bar 18 (that is, giving each bar three minims irrespective of actual
bar lines in the score). It then modulates to the dominant, moving
quickly to its dominant A major, although the orchestral answer
remains no longer strict, moving through A minor to C major, the
voice then returning to D major. Although the da capo section repeats
the first line of the verse, it does not repeat in full the entire first
section of the music, but employs a form of dovetailing: instead of the
usual orchestral repetition of the vocal phrase, the voice takes up, in a
slightly embellished form, adding a crotchet passage reminiscent of its
initial phrase, the original second-violin passage which ends the piece.
The second violin is given a new part over the first violin, and the
remaining instrumental parts are altered, although the harmonies
remain the same. Thus it is only for the final two bars that the voice
and instruments sound together, not with new material but patch-
ing together, so to speak, pieces from within. But by 1684 the

EXAMPLE 3. Cavalli–Faustini, *La Virtù degli strali d'amore* (1642). Act II. 4

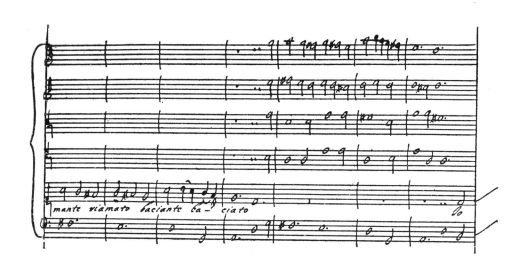

conventional form was established. The aria from *L'incoronatione di Dario*
combines the complete da capo idea, sending the reader back to the
start with a conventional sign, with one of the rare occasions in
which obligato instruments are demanded.[1]

The earlier examples raise an important point in tracing the development of the aria. We have said that the songs included at the

[1] Music example No. 4.

EXAMPLE 4. Freschi–Morselli, *L'incoronatione di Dario* (1684). Act I. 8

end of scenes may be a relic of the old *intermedii*, in which singing interrupted the drama, and that the custom of placing the aria at this
point was later explained on aesthetic grounds. It may seem para-
doxical that the examples should both have been taken from the
middle or opening of a scene. The explanation of the first is simple:
there was the tradition of the *intermedii*, on the one hand, which led to
the strophic aria becoming a part of each scene, a reminder of the old
love of such simple songs introduced in many cases with no feeling
for the continuity of the plot; in fact the strophic structure itself
denied any such possibility breaking up the lengthy recitative. In the
second, on the other hand, there is the need from which the great
arias of the following century derive, the need to emphasize a particular moment in the drama, a purpose for which the strophic song is not
adapted. The most effective means was found to be a form of song too
lyrical to be called recitative and too fragmentary to be called an aria
and which has come to be known as arioso. The style of writing is not
confined to works of the early composers. The example given here is
from *Olimpia Vendicata* (1682). It is a particularly vivid illustration
and one of the few instances of tempo markings in the Contarini scores.

From this arioso style the formal aria developed. The connexion
between it and the da capo example from *La Virtù degli strali d'amore*
can be seen at once. Or, to take a further passage from the opera,[1] the
link appears even more clearly. In this extract the arioso is linked with
a further means of expression, the *recitativo stromentato*, of which Metastasio urges so effective a use in a famous letter to Hasse.[2] The opening

[1] Act III. 4. Music example No. 5.
[2] Vienna 1749. *Letters*, ed. Burney, vol. i, pp. 315 sqq.

EXAMPLE 5. Cavalli–Faustini, *La Virtù degli strali d'amore* (1642). Act III. 4

bars are composed in accompanied recitative which breaks into a lyrical arioso at the change to triple time on the words 'godo in terra beato il paradiso'. Thus the growth of the aria is dependent upon two sources. First, the idea of the song, introduced as relief from the regular story told in recitative, the original structure of a *favola in musica*, from which the formal element is taken; and secondly from the arioso by which the lyrical portions of the text are made to stand out from the ordinary lines. The increasing length of these arioso passages demanded a more formal structure, the text of which librettists arranged to put at the end of the scenes, a position considered more suited to emotional outbursts. But short arioso passages could naturally intercept the recitative for a few bars without holding up the action of the plot in the least; and this method continued as the example from *Olimpia Vendicata* has made clear. In fact the expressive element of the arioso is grafted into the formal structure of an aria so that it really grows out of the recitative with no interruption to the continuity. It is the structure in which Verdi cast his final masterpieces.

Some of the most expressive music in the operas is found in the laments. And in contemporary opinion, too, they were held in high

EXAMPLE 6. Cavalli–Busenello, *La Didone* (1641). Act I. 7

esteem. 'Nelle parte amorose', Ivanovich the well-known librettist wrote, 'vi sono sparsi alcuni lamenti, à quali sarà dirizzata principalmente la curiosità.' And the chromatic ground bass was the basis for the composition of such pieces.[1] One of the most beautiful examples is the lament sung by Hecuba over ruined Troy from Cavalli's *La Didone*.[2] Unlike many other laments the bass in this aria does not overlap the voice part as it does in Purcell's well-known example in *Dido and Aeneas*. Here Cavalli gives the effect of a poignant little sigh by holding over the cadence at the end of each line for one bar after the voice has finished. Pallavicino provides an unusual ground-bass figure made up of arpeggios in *Le amazoni nell' isole fortunate* (1679).[3] Handel used a similar figure later in Agrippina (Act II. 4). The bass gives unity and shape to the aria, made up as it is of nicely balanced four-bar phrases with a little two-bar introduction, the arpeggios simply

[1] For a discussion of the use of the ground bass by Cavalli see Egon Wellesz, *Cavalli und der Stil der venetianischen Oper von 1640–1660*, in Studien zur Musikwissenschaft Beiheft der D.T.Ö., Leipzig, 1913, pp. 38–42. See also Manfred Bukofzer, *Music in the Baroque Era*, London, 1948, pp. 41–42.

[2] Act I. 7. Music example No. 6.   [3] Act III. 1.

Pallavicino **Le amazoni nell' isole fortunate Act III,1. (1679)**

embroider a descending-scale passage typical of such basses. It seems true, then, to say that it is the treatment of a phrase, not its development, that was of importance to the composer. This is particularly noticeable in the aria from *Galieno*[1] (1676). There is a tendency now to introduce each piece with a little accompanying phrase which the voice then repeats, a trait of which Scarlatti was to make good use. About this time, too, the accompaniments seem to lend themselves more naturally to the violoncello. Dent[2] has remarked on the shifting relations between voice and accompanying instrument found in the music of Stradella, who sometimes gives an obvious 'cello phrase to the voice. In general the new treatment of the bass line in the last twenty-five years of the century is most noticeable. This aria from Ziani's *Alcibiade* (1680)[3] is a further instance.

In the lamento the chromatic descent of the bass still keeps its popularity although it is subject to slight variations, generally a move from tonic to dominant for the middle section. An example from *Medea in Atene*[4] in A B A form shows the ground moving to the dominant at bar 11. But it is the bass alone which gives it this form. The first part in the tonic A minor sets to music the first four lines of the verse. The middle and last section are similar in text, with the bass first in the dominant, and returning to the tonic at bar 20. These eight bars are then repeated exactly in the tonic. The aria is rounded off by a five-bar coda, repeating the last phrase of the previous section. The whole is then in strophic form, with two separate quatrains differing in metre and set to different music but linked by a ground. The ground itself as far as key is concerned is an A B A form whilst the voice part in form is A B B1 B2. The libretto makes a separation of the two parts.

Sospiri amorosi
Affanni penosi
Per te fingerò
Se più non vedrò

Che geloso timor
T'agiti l'alma
Ne al seren del tuo cor
Turbi la calma

[1] P. 139.
[2] Edward Dent, *Alessandro Scarlatti*, London, 1905, p. 17.
[3] Act I. 9. Music example No. 7.   [4] Act I. 12. Music example No. 8.

EXAMPLE 7. Ziani–Aureli, *Alcibiade* (1680). Act I. 9

EXAMPLE 8. Zannettini–Aureli, *Medea in Atene* (1675). Act I. 12

But the ground bass overlapping the voice phrases gives the song unity. The ritornello, too, provides a counter-weight to the opening section which the violins repeat. An interesting division of labour in the two upper parts occurs in bars 5 and 6 in which the first violin plays the first half of the phrase occurring in the original voice part, gracing 'fingerò', and the second violin takes up the last part of the phrase.

There is one particular characteristic in the operatic music of Venetian composers which has not as yet received much attention but which may well yield some interesting information as to the methods of composition. Certain melodic phrases, rhetorical formulae they might well be called, briefly touched upon in Chapter IX, recur with surprising regularity. They seem to derive from such books as Caccini's *Nuove Musiche*,[1] in which that composer instructs singers how best to produce the voice in order to achieve the maximum effect. 'Exclamation', he says, 'is the principal means to move the affection, and exclamation properly is no other thing but the slacking of the voice to reinforce it somewhat more.' And the examples which he gives are written to provide suitable phrases for the singer to 'slack' his voice in order that he may obtain a more effective crescendo.

Caccini gives instructions that

in the first minim with a prick, you may tune 'Cor mio', diminishing it by little and little, and in the falling of the crotchet increase the voice with a little more spirit, and it will become an exclamation passionate enough, though in a note that falls but one degree. But much more sprightful will it appear in the word 'deh', by holding of a note that falls not by one degree, as likewise it will become most sweet by the taking of the greater sixth that falls by a leap.

But he does not advise the use of these methods in lively songs or 'airy musics'. In these cases the singing is 'ruled by the air itself'. The exclamations are more suitably employed in the arioso. In fact they grew out of the declamatory style of madrigal of the early seventeenth century in which, as Redlich shows in his biography of Monteverdi, 'the expressive leap of a sixth downwards already comes within the

---

[1] Guilio Caccini, *Le Nuove Musiche*, Florence, 1601. Ai Lettori. (Fac. ed. Rome, 1934.)

scope of the "emotional" '.[1] And the 'emotional' is not confined to leaps of a sixth. For the effect depends partly on the interval itself and partly on the method of producing the voice. In the following example from *Il Ratto delle Sabine* (1680) by Agostini, the tied minim allows the singer to swell the voice before leaping the diminished fifth to emphasize the charm of the Sabine woman. In the first place these unorthodox intervals are used to emphasize the qualities of the text and are not applied to any particular quality such as pain or grief. The passage

that follows from *Gli Amori d'Apollo e di Leucotoe* (1663) contains a double leap in which the ingratitude of Apollo is portrayed by the interval of a ninth.

And the daring leap in a passage from the *Orfeo* (1672) by Sartorio is employed for a like purpose.

A little cadence which often occurs when the singer asks a question seems to be a characteristic of the period and is used particularly by Cesti.

---

[1] Hans Redlich, *Claudio Monteverdi*, O.U.P., 1952, p. 73.

And by Sartorio in *L'Orfeo* (1673) Act. I. 10.

The cadence on 'calma serena' is particularly effective after the display of gorgia on the 'godrà' that precedes it in the example from *Argia*.

Venetian scores are not remarkable for such elaborate vocal fireworks. Little scale-passages, trills, and repeated notes used as illustrations to the text are found fairly often. But the florid singing such as

became common later is seldom used, although an exception must be made for the aria from Freschi's *L'incoronatione di Dario*, Act I. 8.[1]

There is, of course, a certain artificiality about these figures. They need to be studied according to the conventions of the time before they can be thoroughly understood. For they are part of the rhetoric upon which music depended so largely for its appreciation. It would need a detailed study of many scores, both operatic and instrumental,

---

[1] Music example No. 4.

before it were possible to give an analysis such as Pirro has been able to do for the works of Bach in his *L'Esthétique de J. S. Bach*, although there can be no doubt that such a study would prove a fascinating and fruitful work and do perhaps more to help us understand the creative mind of the seventeenth-century musician than anything else. For as Professor Oakeshott says, 'We do not begin to learn our native language by learning the alphabet, or by learning its grammar; we do not begin by learning words, but words in use; we do not begin (as we begin in reading) with what is easy and go on to what is more difficult; we do not begin at school, but in the cradle: and what we say springs always from our manner of speaking.'[1] In music we must, then, understand, above all, the contemporary idiom before it is possible to appreciate the meaning of the sounds. The few examples that have been given here do no more than indicate the possibility that certain figures may have become so inbred in a composer's mind that by unconscious association they came naturally as the most direct means of expressing his thoughts. Once such figures become part of contemporary idiom they have no need to remain chained to words, they can pass from vocal to instrumental music and keep the same powerful effect. But in such a cursory glance into the subject as has been done here we must confine ourselves to the study of operatic technique, the field in which the rhetorical musical devices were most prolifically used in the early stages of the development. The strange harmonies, leaps of diminished and augmented intervals, crescendo and diminuendo of the voice in isolated phrases, had to be seen in their context for their force to become fully apparent. The dangers inherent in such a practice are obvious. Music could be required to express more than was musically possible. And the ingenious could put into compositions ideas that could not be heard but only seen from the printed notes, with the composer's, it might almost be said author's, explanation alongside. The correspondence of Huygens[2] shows that this

---

[1] *Political Education*, Inaugural Lecture, University of London. Cambridge, 1951.

[2] *Musique et musiciens au XVIIe siècle*, ed. W. J. A. Jonckbloet et J. P. N. Land, Leyden, 1882. p. lxxxiii, Mersenne to Huygens, 29 November 1640: 'En troisieme lieu, l'on doit remarquer que ce n'est pas à chaque diction qu'il faut avoir esgard, pour luy donner l'accent ou le mouvement de la passion. Car il faut premierement voir à quoy bute tout le sujet du discours compris dans l'air; et puis ce que contient chaque periode. De sorte que chaque diction considerée en son particulier n'est pas plus considerable que l'une des pierres d'un bastiment: important fort peu quelle place elle tienne dans la muraille, pourveu que le mur soit ferme, et qu'il ait la force que l'architecte desire.'

danger was appreciated amongst European intellectuals as early as 1640. It may be that the social setting of Venice, where cultivated appreciation joined with popular taste in a communal entertainment, was a major factor in keeping the art of singing a musical rather than a literary exercise.

The Chorus and Concerted Music

The slight musical value of concerted pieces in Venice has been sufficiently stressed by such authorities as Goldschmidt and Wellesz. But there are two points in particular which emerge with relevance to this subject from a study and comparison of the scores with the librettos that until now have not been stressed. It appears that the *choro* so lavishly used in the librettos, especially in early operas, is in fact rather a *Bewegungschor* which danced as well as sang and was given, on that account, simple music which such a body could more easily manage. Furthermore, it seems that the large number of attendants on the chief characters in the later historical plots were marked in the librettos 'personaggi muti', who were required to act as crowd and were part of the *décor*. They were obliged to sing in the opening scene, but the extreme brevity and simplicity of their music hardly amounted to more than a shout, after which they became, as it were, stage props, who supported by their number and presence the dignity of the prince to whom they were attached. Thus, in spite of the lack of chorus in the musical sense, the theatres employed a large number of *comparse*, described as the *choro*. Thus the libretto of Cavalli's *La Didone* (1641) lists

> Choro di Damigelle Cartaginesi
> di Cacciatori
> de Troiani
> di Ninfe Marine

in addition to the already large cast. And in *Il Medoro* (1658) by Luzzo we find

> Choro di Mori Indiani con Medoro
> di Damigelle con Angelica
> di Damigelle con Auristella
> di Eunochi con Miralba
> di Soldati Assiri con Brimante
> di Soldati con Leomede
> di Guerrieri Circassi con Sacripante.

Yet, if we look at the position of these groups in the scores, we find it to be of slight importance. In the *La Didone* the chorus of Trojans opens Act I with a simple call to arms for two sopranos, alto, two tenors, bass, and continuo 'tutti con radoppio d'instrumenti' who sing 'Armi Enea, 'diamo all' armi', which is repeated twice in Scene 1. In Act II. 2 and 3 the girls' chorus is present on the stage, but is silent. Equally, in Scene 5 the sea-nymphs are silent; it is worth mentioning here that the intervening scene is sufficiently long to allow of a quick change of costume. In Scene 6 the Graces are introduced in the libretto and given a quatrain which is cut in the score. However, the chorus of hunters are given four verses in Act III. 3 of a more elaborate nature than usual. The music is in the style of a popular villotta[1] with a last-line refrain, 'tu tu tu al cingiale, al cingiale'. This chorus for alto, two tenors, and bass, needs singers able to undertake solos; for, of the last three stanzas, the bass sings two and a tenor one. The Trojan chorus reappears in Scene 6 in the libretto, but is cut in the score.

Equally in *Medoro* the Assyrian soldiers and Moorish Indians are silent in Act I. 1, as are the Circassian warriors in Scene 3. The remaining members of the chorus are not mentioned, although in Act III. 21 we find 'voce di applauso popolare'. Yet in the score Luzzo has written five bars for instruments in $\frac{3}{2}$ time marked 'ritornello'. Later the number of *comparse*, as they are called, increased, but numbers of them are, as in fact they always had been, labelled 'personaggi muti or taciti', numbering sometimes, according to the *Mercure Galant*, up to fifty persons for the escort of a royal and imperial figure. However, compared to the huge company needed in Melani's *Ercole in Tebe*, produced at the Pergola theatre in Florence, these numbers are not great although they increase later in the century. The *Mercure Galant*[2] tells of a battle-scene opening an opera in which 'plus de cent Personnes estoient engagées dans ce combat. Il duroit pres de demy-heure'. And again,[3] it says that 'lorsqu'un Empereur ou un Roi entre sur un théâtre il est toujours accompagné de 30–40 ou 50 Gardes qui sont autour de lui'. Vespasiano[4] has nine characters in the plot and, in addition to a

---

[1] Alfred Einstein, *The Italian Madrigal*, p. 343. He mentions the dance-like nature of these songs which could fit in with the theory of the ballet-chorus.

[2] *Mercure Galant*, April 1679.   [3] Ibid., March 1683.

[4] *Il Vespasiano*. Drama per musica nel nuovo Teatro Grimano di S. Giò. Grisostomo, Venice, 1678. Text, Corradi; music, Pallavicino. The growing taste for huge casts is illustrated by the production of this opera in Ferrara, 1687, advertised 'in questa terza impressione aggiuntove di nuovo Ariette, e Personaggi non inserte nell' altre antecedenti'.

hundred *comparse*, a list of mythological figures requiring machines to bring them on, and eight choruses. Yet they were not considered as musical entities but rather as a *corps de ballet*, often marked as silent characters. The list in the libretto reads:

Giunone su Carro tirato da due Pavoni.
Cibelle su Carro tirato da due Leoni.
Fetonte su Carro tirato da due Cavalli vivi.
Giove su l'Aquila.
Il Po.
Apollo sul Cavallo Pegaseo in cima del Monte Parnasso, col
Choro delle Muse.

Personaggi muti.
Choro di Cavalieri, Paggi, e Guerrieri con Vespasiano.
    di Guerrieri con Tito.
    d'Alabardieri con Domitiano.
    di Soldate con Attilio.
    di Dame con Arricida.
    delle Aure (breezes) con Giunone.
    di Ninfe con il Po.
    di Pastori con Cibelle, with 'balli di Paggi, lottatori e di varie persone
        in terra, in aria, e in acqua'.

Unlike the size of the orchestra, which can be explained as dependent largely upon finance, the size of the chorus is governed, if ultimately by finance, more immediately by taste. The audience in Venice was drawn from all classes and nationalities who came to see a *dramma in musica* or a *favola per musica*. And the plots themselves were concerned exclusively with the emotions and actions of the principal characters. The points of repose, which are given to a lyrical chorus in classical drama, are here given to the principal characters in their arias around which, in common with the scenic marvels, popular interest revolved. And the impressario demanded music suitable to attract an audience with those tastes. To that degree, in order to pay the singers, expense may be said to have contributed to the absence of a chorus. But the prime reasons lay in the interest in the aria and singers which claimed all attention. The 'occasional' performances at courts were a different matter; for there, unlike a public entertainment given nightly, for which the convenience of the audience had to be considered and which, apart from the need to appeal to popular taste, had to be restricted tò certain hours from the point of view of the performers, even though they were long,[1] the dimensions of the festivity could be extended to include elaborate numbers for solo characters as well as chorus, ballet, and machines. In the circumstances it is not surprising that both producers and composers in Venice should have cut down on the cumbersome body of singers. It was easier for the one to create a magnificent crowd-effect without the bother of a chorus master, and more profitable for the other to compose for solo voices, contenting the chorus with short exclamations, 'alla caccia', 'all' armi', 'viva', 'vittoria', and so on, which could be sung by almost any member of the crowd. Therefore, although the size of what is termed the chorus in the lists of the casts increases in the later operas, it is, in fact, only the crowd or *comparse* which grows, as a liking for battle or other grand scenes requiring a lavish stage-effect necessary to the historical plots becomes the fashion. But its duty is simply to warn or cheer the main characters according to circumstances. However, the return of Cavalli from Paris in 1662 appears to have increased the interest in the chorus, for we find him using it with a certain dramatic effect, employing two contrasting sections in *Scipione Africano* during Act I. 2, in which the crowd watches a gladiatorial contest. The full four-part chorus with continuo sing:

> 'Ferite, uccidite
> No, no, non timete'

Whilst a soprano chorus in two parts with continuo answers:

> 'Mostrando valore
> Con Cloria si more'
>
> *Full chorus*: 'Feroti pugnate
> Severi svenate'
>
> *Sopranos*: 'Ch'un animo forte
> Disprezza la morte.'

Although such an arrangement is short, it has a greater dramatic value than the usual calls to arms, but is sufficiently compact to enable the untrained *comparse* of Venice to sing it. A further example from Act II of his *Pompeo Magno* (1666) shows the homophonic character of the pieces, the effect of which depended not upon the music but upon the grandeur of the scene itself. Two princes, drawn from the courtiers, sing the middle section.

---

[1] Evelyn left the opera at two in the morning.

The chorus that appears in this opening-display scene is seldom heard again during the operas. The crowd splits up into the followers of the main protagonists and appears with them throughout in the capacity of *personaggi muti*.

In the opening chorus from P. A. Ziani's *L'Annibale in Capua* (1661), in which Hannibal enters on an elephant, the victory-shouts last longer than usual but they illustrate the simple form such pieces took. The trumpet-like figurations are typically symbolic of the occasion.

Further indication of the local dislike of choral music can be deduced from the unsuccessful attempts to imitate foreign styles or the reverse in cases where foreign works have been adapted to Venetian taste. From the visits of Cavalli and the Italian designer Torelli to France, and from the interchange of composers and works between Vienna and Venice and other Italian cities, it is certain that in Venice the habits of all foreign opera-houses were well known. And the constant references to the latest Venetian productions in the *Mercure Galant* show that it was a reciprocated interest. However, an interesting manuscript in the Contarini collection proves that even detailed study of the latest Paris operas was possible in Venice. The score of Lully's *Thésée* which had its first performance at Saint-Germain on New Year's Day 1675, although it was not printed until 1688,[1] is to be found as a manuscript in the Marciana, copied by the same hand as the manuscript of Zannettini's *Medea in Atene*, first performed on 14 December of the same year. There is no indication, and it is unlikely for practical reasons of stage management, that the Lully opera ever had a performance in Venice. And we do not know which of the two the scribe copied first. But, since the *Medea* shows an unusually well-developed use of the chorus and has a certain modified similarity to the *Thésée*, it is possible that Zannettini was influenced by the French work. The sinfonia is in the French style with a fugatto second section, in itself a common practice, but the fugatto is imitated in the prologue by a chorus of gods, goddesses, and orchestra unusual and on a grander scale than the ordinary Venetian prologue, although reminiscent of a

---

[1] Alfred Loewenberg, op. cit., p. 29.

EXAMPLE 9. Cavalli–Persiani, *Le Nozze di Teti e di Peleo* (1639). Act. I. 1

much older opera by Cavalli, *Il Ciro* (1654).[1] Yet, in spite of this con-
jectured attempt to imitate the chorus of Lully, the result was not
popular, for it is not the prototype of further ventures but a more or
less isolated example. Conversely, Ziani's *La Schiava fortunata* (1674)
has a choral finale in the Austrian edition, but in the Venice manuscript the quartet is altered to a solo.

Equally neglected in Venice are passages for concerted singing,

[1] Egon Wellesz, *Cavalli und der Stil der venetianischen Oper 1640–1660*, pp. 79–91.

duets, trios, and larger numbers. They are found mostly in the earlier Cavalli works, particularly in the pastoral-epic operas into which a number of mythological and magical characters could be introduced. Cavalli's *Le Nozze di Teti e di Peleo*[1] (1639) has a sextet in the first scene, the singers being characters from Greek mythology. Between the chorus of soloists there is an instrumental interlude, a *chiamata alla caccia*, and a similar scene later in the opera is written for a *choro di Cavalieri*.[2] But, since the number of parts is identical, there is no reason why the same cast should not sing in both. In a chorus of this nature which combines with the instrumental ritornello the character of a ballet, the economic and administrative difficulties play an insignificant part. One further example of a quartet who could dance at the same time comes from *La Virtù degli Strali d'Amore* (1642). This opera has a large cast including choruses of nymphs, magicians, silent spirits, nereids, and sea gods. In one scene the magicians torment the bewitched prince Darete.[3] And his shrieks of 'ahi' punctuate the chorus. 'Viene per l'aere Ericlea accompagnata da Maghe amiche sopra il dorso de' mostri a tormentare con le faci Darete fratello di Cleria da lei incantato in quella selva dentro una pianta.' But the stage directions continue: 'Dato fine a tormenti formano un ballo con atti di scherno verso Darete', a further indication that the chorus were members of a *corps de ballet* as well.

From this opera it is possible to illustrate a duet.[4] Again, its length is unusual. For the most part such pieces consist of short phrases, 't'adoro' answers 'ti stringo', and in concert the voices conclude 'che dolce diletto' or some such cliché. But as a serious form the duet, except in early works, can scarcely be said to have had a place in Venice. In fact, the position is clear from a comparison between Cesti's setting of Moniglia's libretto, *La Schiava fortunata*, written for Vienna, and the opera in the form altered to suit conditions in Venice by M. A. Ziani and Corradi in 1674. The concerted pieces in the libretto are cut entirely and the lines given to a soloist.

The absence of concerted pieces becomes a weakness in the structure of Italian opera which is not set right until the following century. It is, however, instructive to see that the Italian attitude towards them was

[1] Act I. 1. Music example No. 9.
[2] Hugo Goldschmidt, *Studien zur Geschichte der italienischen Oper im 17. Jahrhundert*, pp. 391–401.
[3] Act I. 10. Music example No. 10.   [4] Act III. 15. Music example No. 11.

EXAMPLE 10. Cavalli–Faustini, *La Virtù degli Strali d'Amore* (1642). Act. I. 10

EXAMPLE 11. Cavalli–Faustini, *La Virtù degli Strali d'Amore* (1642). Act. III. 15

intentional and not altogether the result of an inability to write on a large scale. For Monteverdi's librettist Badovero[1] considered that the chorus was unnecessary and tedious in a play sung throughout. He suggests that it should be used as a *ballo* as in fact, as we have seen, it became.

[1] *Le Nozze d'Enea con Lavinia* printed *argomento et scenario* in which Badovero explains the changes he has made in Virgil's original to suit the taste of the times. It is an interesting testimony to the aims of an early librettist.

The Orchestra

During the seventeenth century it becomes possible to speak of the opera orchestra in the modern sense of the word. It begins to take the shape of an organized body of players situated in front of the stage; the haphazard choice of instruments, because they are available, begins to give place to a more careful use as the composer realizes the qualities of tone and even association by which particular instruments suited certain situations. The foundations of the orchestra can be seen in the advice given by Marco de Gagliano to a producer that the instruments should be placed so that they can see the singers and thus keep time more easily.[1] They assume an essential place in the production and are not pushed into a convenient corner as a luxury, such as was still the case in England in the middle of the century where the 'Musick was above in a loover hole railed about and covered with sarcenetts to conceal them'.[2] Yet here, too, even in the earlier part of the century,[3] the orchestra was sometimes to be found seated in front of the stage. But in the Venetian public opera-houses its position was consolidated. The *Mercure Galant*[4] mentions that the necks of the theorbos hid the stage from the first tier of boxes, a fact that no doubt explains why these were less fashionable than the upper rows. One of Coronelli's engravings of the theatre S. Giovanni Grisostomo shows the orchestra in front of the stage.[5] And the *Mercure Galant*[6] points out that the players can be of either sex, a habit that created the famous female orchestras at Venice in the subsequent century. Its size no doubt varied from theatre to theatre, but in S. Giovanni Grisostomo it numbered forty

[1] Angelo Solerti, op. cit., vol. ii, p. 69. Preface from *Dafne* (1608): 'Primieramente avvertiscasi che gli strumenti che devono accompagnare le voci sole, sieno situati in luogo da vedere in viso i recitanti, acciò che meglio sentendosi, vadano unitamente.'

[2] State Papers Dom. Ser. 1655–6, vol. cxxviii, p. 108.

[3] W. A. Keith, 'The Designs for the first moveable scenery on the English public stage', *Burlington Magazine*, vol. xxv, 1914; see the plan for *Florimene* (1635).

[4] *Mercure Galant*, March 1683: 'Ceux du second rang sont les plus recherchez, et entre ceux-cy, on préfère ceux du fond qui regardent le théâtre en face, où sont ordinairement les Loges des ambassadeurs parceque ... le Manche des Theorbes de l'orchestre cache toujours quelque chose de la veüe.'   [5] Henri Prunières, *Cavalli et l'opéra vénitien*, pl. vii.   [6] *Mercure Galant*, August 1677.

players.[1] However, before the public opera-houses became established in popular estimation, the numbers of players were not so large and do not compare with the orchestras employed in the royal and princely households. A comparison between the orchestra used in Monteverdi's two operas written for Venice and his works written for the Gonzaga court makes it clear. *Il ritorno d'Ulisse in patria* and *L'incoronatione di Poppea* are scored for strings and continuo alone, whereas the earlier works employ richer and more varied combinations.[2]

However, the last thirty years of the century witnessed the increase in number and variety of the public opera-house orchestras. The forty players for *Il Nerone*, about which the *Mercure Galant* spoke, consisted of 'flûtes douces, trompetes, timbales, violas et violons'. In the scores themselves the instruments are seldom specified. Flutes form no part of the orchestra in the *Codices Contariniani*. An aria from *L'Eraclio* (1671) opens 'al fragor di trombe, e timpani'. And productions in the Contarini theatre at Piazzola use, for example in Freschi's *Berenice Vendicativa* (1680), flutes and organ, whilst his *Olimpia Vendicata* given in Venice (San Angelo, 1682) requires the organ. Goldschmidt[3] gives an early use of instruments in *Le Nozze di Teti e di Peleo* (1639), in which the chorus (Act I. 4) is accompanied by 'Corni e Tambori'. A similar example from the same opera is reproduced in music example No. 9. Horns are not mentioned elsewhere in these manuscripts. Yet it is possible that where musicians appeared on the stage, generally for some procession or crowd scene, they provided suitable music for wind or brass. Amongst the cast in *Scipione Africano* musicians are mentioned. They played at a gladiatorial contest in the first act.[4] The sinfonia to this opera is scored, according to the clefs, for two violins, viola, tenor violin, and violoncello. At this time the bass viol was not in general use in Italy. In fact, writing from Lucca, the home of the celebrated librettist Sbarra, in 1657, Thomas Hill says 'the instrumental music is much better than I expected. The organ and violin they are masters of, but the bass-viol they have not at all in use and

---

[1] *Mercure Galant*, August 1679: 'Quarante Instruments des meilleurs qu'on eust pû trouver, servoient à la Simphonie.'

[2] Jack Westrup, 'Monteverdi and the orchestra', *M. & L.*, vol. xxi, July 1940.

[3] Hugo Goldschmidt, *Studien zur Geschichte der italienischen Oper*, pp. 391–401.

[4] *Scipione Africano*. Drama per musica nel Teatro a SS. Giò. e Paolo, 1664. Text, Minato; music, Cavalli. 'Al suono di varii stromenti, li Gladiatori girano l'Anfiteatro gettando in aria gl'Elmi, e l'Haste in forma di gioco.'

to supply its place they have the bass violin with four strings, and use it as we do the viol.'[1] The most usual stringed instruments were of the violin family and not the viols as is logical from the proximity of Venice to Cremona and from the need for a powerful tone in the opera-houses. It is interesting to note the fairly constant scoring of the inner part, as we might imagine, amongst the alto and tenor violins. But, although the parts are written at times both in the alto and tenor clefs or divided on the one alto stave, the lower part never goes below the C of the viola's fourth string. Professor Westrup mentions this to be the case in Monteverdi's *Orfeo*.[2] And it is also true of the Venetian scores. Accordingly, we may with equal reason assume that violas played both parts; and additional support can be seen in 'sinfonia con trombe', from Partenio's *Genserico* (Act III. 18). The mention of the instruments by name itself in this piece is exceptional. Two trumpet parts are marked 'T' on the left of the two upper staves, the two upper-string parts, written on one stave, marked 'Viol', and the two inner parts, equally on one stave in the alto clef, are marked 'Viole', which would support the view that the viola was in use in the orchestra. The theorbo certainly played a prominent part in the orchestral pit and helped fill in the continuo.

The orchestra was used primarily in the sinfonia and ritornello. It was brought in to accompany the aria in many cases, and to give a special emphasis to certain points in the recitative. The sinfonia served not only as the traditional introduction to an opera,[3] little more than a few perfunctory chords in earlier works very often, but compositions marked as such were inserted as interludes in the work itself. Such interludes as the 'sinfonia di viole' in Cavalli's *Le Nozze di Teti e di Peleo*,[4] which is heard in answer to an appeal for sweet music by Peleo to assuage the bitter pangs of love:

Tocca dunque o Chirone corde sublimi
E mille suoni in un sol suono esprimi.

[1] W. H., A. F., and A. E. Hill, *Antonio Stradivari. His life and work (1644–1737)*, London 1902, p. 110. The popularity of the instrument can be gathered from the school of violoncello composers which flourished in northern Italy towards the end of the century, the works of whom find mention in Robert Haas, *Die Estensischen Musikalien*, p. 31.
[2] Jack Westrup, op. cit., p. 233.
[3] Angelo Solerti, op. cit., p. 69. Preface to *Dafne*: 'Innanzi al calar della tenda, per render attenti gli uditori, sonisi una sinfonia composta di diversi istromenti.'
[4] Music example No. 12 and Wellesz, *Cavalli und der Stil der venetianischen Oper von 1640–1660*, p. 50.

EXAMPLE 12. Cavalli–Persiani, *Le Nozze di Teti e di Peleo* (1639). Act. II. 6

The blank bars in this score are a reminder of the habits of the day in which so much was left to the skill of the instrumentalist and to conventions common to all. But the care with which the instrumentation is marked shows a growing appreciation for orchestral colour. The rich tones of the violas were particularly suitable for the music needed on such an occasion. This piece provides an interesting parallel with the grave sinfonia in Act III of Monteverdi's *Orfeo* which Professor Westrup suggests may have been scored for violas.[1] It is written in the soprano, mezzo-soprano, alto, tenor, and bass clefs which in itself is no proof that violas were used in each, for as a guide to instrumentation clefs are inconclusive and, as in the *Orfeo*, it is possible to play the upper parts on the violin. But the indication 'di viole' and the fact that the upper parts are within easy compass of the viola in the score suggest the possibility. In both cases their use would give the required solemn effect. The brilliant tones of the violins would be more suitable to a scene such as can be found in *Vespasiano*[2] (1678) in which Domitian attempts to rape his brother's wife Arracida as she is seated beside him at a banquet with his officers and their mistresses. As the food is carried in the composer gives directions for a 'bizzara sinfonia di stromenti': the curious effects of the string parts may well be the

musical counterpart to the debauch on the stage, an example of the application of the *veresimile* in opera. The opera was popular in Italy, was repeated in Venice in 1680, and on numerous occasions elsewhere.[3]

[1] Jack Westrup, op. cit., pp. 233–4.   [2] Act I. 13. Music example No. 13.
[3] Alfred Loewenberg, op. cit.

EXAMPLE 13. Pallavicino–Corradi, *Il Vespasiano* (1678). Act. I. 13

Sinfonias for trumpets and orchestra became popular, as stories from medieval history were taken as subjects for so many plots. They are generally associated with the more splendid scenes but are, of course, harmonically simple and restricted to the key of D major. It may be that the re-found love of display was the outcome of an influence from Vienna where the magnificent *Pomo d'Oro* had been given by Cesti in 1667, for subsequent to that date these scenes are greatly increased. A composite opera, *Iphide Greca* (1671), contains a 'sinfonia con trombe' and five-part strings in the tradition of Lully in the middle of the first act: it is repeated three times, each time louder as the crowd draws near.[1] Trumpets, used as concerto instruments, are found contrasted against a body of strings;[2] and there is one example in the Contarini MSS. of an aria[3] in which a solo violin and trumpet form a little

[1] The Viennese influence is borne out by a note in the preface: 'Questo nobilissimo drama, se ne passa dal soglio de Cesari à dilettar il genio de gli Adriatici eroi.' (Oscar Sonneck, *Library of Congress Catalogue of Opera Librettos printed before 1800*, Washington, 1914, p. 640.)

[2] Act I. 3. Music example No. 14.   [3] Music example No. 4.

EXAMPLE 14. Legrenzi–Noris, *Totila* (1677). Act. I. 3

concerto with the voice. It is interesting to notice how the figurations suitable for one medium are at this time transferred to another. The violin figures in the sinfonia for *Medea in Atene* (1675) derive from the vocal technique for the *trillo* and *gruppo* described by Caccini in the *Nuove Musiche*, whilst farther on in the scene there is a passage in the 'stile concitato' in the accompaniment to an aria during the Athenian Games. But the imitation is two-sided. If instruments imitate the voice to begin with, the voice soon hopes to imitate what are obviously instrumental phrases. This is particularly noticeable in the cadenzas of the great eighteenth-century castratos. But in a small way these two examples show a distant echo of trumpet figurations.

Perhaps the distinction between the instrumental interlude and the overture, although both are called 'sinfonia' in the score, can best be made in terms of the descriptive or subjective values of the one which are absent from the other. The 'sinfonia avanti l'opera', or overture, possessed characteristics such as the clearly defined phrases contrasting tonic and dominant, and a division into two or more contrasting sections. The opening sinfonia from Cavalli's *Scipione Africano*[1] is representative of this type. The first section, repeated, opens with minim chords for three bars followed by a further three-bar phrase with the dominating rhythm of the piece. The two phrases are now repeated

[1] Music example No. 15.

EXAMPLE 15. Cavalli–Minato, *Scipione Africano* (1664). Opening sinfonia

in the dominant G major extended for a further four bars, moving to A major, the submediant. The concluding section of the first part is a variation of bar 4 repeated until the tonic is reached. The section ends with a full close in C major. The second part, in $\frac{3}{4}$ time, is divided into two phrases of five bars each, starting in the dominant G and passing through D, returning to G for the first section. The concluding harmonies pass through G D A minor and back to the tonic C. The bass rhythm is constant throughout both phrases, whilst the viola retains a continual dotted crotchet ♩. ♪ ♩ rhythm. The remaining parts employ this rhythm in the first phrase but in the second follow the bass. This section is also repeated, making the sinfonia a movement of sixty bars in which a good deal of variety is obtained; it shows a considerable development over the sinfonia for *La Virtù degli strali d'amore* (1642) which, although in three sections of five bars, each repeated, consists of the block chord of A major reiterated with ever-increasing strength in these rhythms ♩ ♩ ♩ ♩ ♩ ♩ ♩ ♩ ♩ ♩ ♩ ♩ ♩ ♩ ♩ ♩ ♩ ♩ ♩ ♩ ♩ ♩ ♩, an effective device to compel silence. Yet the introduction to an opera was more than a means to attract the attention of the audience. It was a definite part of the performance. In Cavalli's *L'Ormindo* (1641) the sinfonia acts as a ritornello joining the various recitative passages of the prologue. Yet, it is called sinfonia throughout. Therefore, if the orchestral introduction is an integral part of the prologue, it reflects, at any rate to some extent, the interest felt for the actual music of these performances as distinct from the scenic marvels in that the piece was more than a device to quell the chatter of the audience. Although these instrumental introductions followed no absolute rule, the form, generally speaking, was in what has come to be considered the French style. The sinfonia to Pallavicino's *Il Demetrio* (1666) is marked 'grave', 'affetuoso', 'presto', 'adagio'. Few are as elaborate as that, although each of these sections consists of a few bars only. Yet the arrangement is always along similar lines, opening with a stately movement. But the subsequent sections are left to the composers' choice. There is not always a return to a slow movement. For example, the sinfonia preceding Cesti's *Argia* (1655) opens with a grave movement in $\frac{2}{2}$ followed by a fugato in $\frac{3}{2}$ time repeated, and ends with a quick movement in $\frac{4}{4}$ time, whereas Cavalli's *L'Erismena* of the same year is in A B A form. It is interesting to note that this opera, revised and performed again in 1670 retains the original sinfonia altering the key from C to D major; hence we can see that, in this matter, taste had not altered, although the desire for additional arias is marked in that opera. Even in Pallavicino's celebrated *Le Amazoni nell' isole fortunate* (1679), a lavish Piazzola production, the 'sinfonia avanti levar della tenda' is a simple three-movement piece for two violins and continuo marked 'largo', 'sarabande', 'grave'.

The instrumental ritornello, another important orchestral section, is not, as in Monteverdi's *Orfeo*, a piece recurrent throughout the drama, but is attached to the particular aria, either connecting the verses, or as an interlude before the action re-starts. As a rule, although there are many exceptions, it does not bear thematic relation to the aria itself. It may be set in the same key. But, unlike the normal sinfonia, it is definitely attached to the aria, returning between each verse. In fact, Dr. Wellesz points out[1] that the difference between the sinfonia and ritornello, at any rate in the earlier operas up till about 1660, lies not in the music but in the production. And it is a conclusion which finds support from further research. For example, the opening sinfonia from Cavalli's *Gli amori d'Apollo e di Dafne*[2] is followed without a break by the identical piece in double time marked 'ritornello', which makes it reasonable to suppose, especially when we find that the quick ritornello connects various parts of the recitative in the prologue, although thematically absolutely distinct from them, that, in the ritornello, some sort of regrouping of characters or action took place. Again, the ritornello in the music example No. 2, from the same opera, bears no relation to the strophic song the verses of which it serves to link. However, in itself, it shows an interesting equality amongst the three parts, opening with a canon at the fifth for the two violins in G minor which occupies the first nine bars, ending in the relative major. The second part, of ten bars, is led off by the second violin in a further canon for the violin and bass, in a return to the tonic, G minor; this part is itself a modification of the original canon, using bars 1 and 2 for six bars in a sequential figure whilst the first violin imitates the second violin at the third above, after the initial figure is announced. Passages unconnected with the strophic song itself but, this time, less elaborate, consisting of a few bars, but scored for five

---

[1] Egon Wellesz, op. cit., pp. 47–48.
[2] Ibid., p. 60. The sinfonia is quoted in full but the change from ¢ to ₵ is not marked 'ritornello' as it is in the Marciana MS.

EXAMPLE 16. Cavalli–Faustini, *L'Egisto* (1643). Act. I. 2

instruments, are found in Cavalli's *Didone* (1641) and *Egisto*[1] (1643), in music examples Nos. 1 and 16. But the characteristics of the voice part are incorporated into the ritornello. The form of appoggiatura in the *Didone* and the flowing crotchets in the *Egisto* find their echo in the instrumental pieces.

However, the tendency for the ritornello to echo the aria is more marked as the century progresses. In Cesti's *La Dori*[2] (1663) the descending-scale passage with which the aria opens is echoed in the ritornello. This manuscript is in a particularly clear and beautiful hand although the copyist has mistakenly written the voice part in the tenor rather than the alto clef. But he corrects himself by writing 'alla 5a' in the margin. The placing of the notes which are not correct in relation to the other clefs makes it difficult to read; the first semiquaver F in bar 5 for the second violin is no doubt a mistake for A. A ground bass can be the link between the ritornello and aria as in the music examples Nos. 7 and 8. But in these examples, too, the orchestra bears a close resemblance to the aria to which it is attached.

But it seems clear that the musical connexion between the ritornello and the aria is a comparatively late development, and that, in origin, it

[1] Act I. 2.   [2] Act II. 9. Music example No. 17.

EXAMPLE 17. Cesti–Apolloni, *La Dori* (1663). Act II. 9

followed or interspersed strophes of an aria for extra musical reasons. In fact, it is only from the moment when its link with the aria becomes thematic, the accidental result of its position in the production, that we are able to distinguish it from the sinfonia. The sinfonia itself was either a piece of music with which the performance opened, in which case it followed the style of the French overture or it was introduced as an 'occasional' piece into the action and depended for its character upon its place in the plot and the kind of responses required from the audience.

The use of the orchestra in the *ballo* is difficult to assess. It must have accompanied the dancing as it accompanied the regrouping of the singers in the ritornellos. Yet the Italians were so casual in the treatment of the dance that the music is seldom included in the scores. The indication 'segue il ballo' suffices for them. It was customary to have a *ballo* after the first and second act although its appearance is more usual in the libretto than in the score. The habit derived from the *intermedii* written as *entr'acte* entertainment at court,[1] although the old *intermedii* were on a far larger scale than the usual *ballo*. But they are certainly the parent.

The dances are always connected with the plot. And a scene is chosen to end an act which would be suitable for a character dance. These have no political significance as their French counterparts had, according to Paquot's interesting study of the matter.[2] They were only a device to finish an act conveniently and to urge on the audience to enthusiasm. Busenello's *Didone* (1641) shows relics of the older *intermedio* in an elaborate picture of the Trojan navy with sails set, crossing the stage, which ends the first act,[3] whilst the second finishes with a 'ballo di Mori Affricani'. Sometimes a dance scene was included within an act. There is an example in *Pompeo Magno*[4], during which occurs 'un ballo di Cavalli vivi con Cavallieri sopra al suono di Trombe, e d'altri stromenti', whereas the act itself ends with 'il ballo di otto Impazzati', each pair of which present music, painting, alchemy,

---

[1] Angelo Solerti, *Gli Albori del Melodramma*, Milan, vol. ii, pp. 15 sqq.; vol. iii, pp. 205 sqq.

[2] Marcel Paquot, *Les Étrangers dans les divertissements de la cour*, Paris, 1932. On p. 131 he points out the corollary: 'Les divertissements chorégraphiques représentés pendant la période où le genre subit l'influence des œuvres italiennes, sont pauvres d'allusions politiques.'

[3] 'Qui passa l'Armata Troiana à vele gonfie, e finisce il Primo Atto.'

[4] *Pompeo Magno*. Drama per musica nel Teatro à S. Salvatore. Venice, 1666. Text, Nic. Minato; music, Fr. Cavalli. Act I. 4.

and poetry. The tradition continues throughout the century. An act of *Alcibiade*[1] ends in the workshop belonging to Prassitele and the *ballo* is performed by 'scultori discepoli'. Later, further evidence shows that Venice tended to adapt customs from the multitude of tourists who came to see her once unique spectacles. Dances are found with specific titles, 'alla Francese' or 'alla Spagnola',[2] instead of the old villanella or moresca which by then had ceased to have any local significance. But our knowledge is limited to these hints in the librettos, for the ballet music itself is still unknown to us.

[1] *L'Alcibiade*. Drama per musica nel famosissimo Teatro Grimano à SS. Giò. e Paolo, Venice, 1680. Text, Aureli; music, M. A. Ziani. Act II.

[2] For a particular example see *Publio Elio pertinace*. Drama per musica da rappresentarsi nel Teatro Vendramino di San Salvatore, Venice, 1684. Text, Ab. P. d'Averara; music, Legrenzi.

The Relations between Composer and Librettist

The newly recognized power of music to extract a deeper meaning from the texts, to express finer shades of feeling than the words could themselves indicate, had a far-reaching effect on the relationship between poet and musician. The text of an opera became of great significance, since the music had only the one aim, that of enhancing the words. The words came to be regarded as the design and the music the colour. The result of this relationship tended to make the poet the senior partner. And, in spite of the apparent insipidness of the texts, that emphasis was to hold good for most of the seventeenth century. The composer therefore became the handmaid, to some extent, to the poet. Of course, sixteenth-century madrigalists, Rore, Wert, or Lassus, of whom Einstein can write 'he does not paint: he sets the ethos of the poem to music',[1] and Marenzio, for example, had aimed at expressing the texts of their madrigals as, indeed, Monteverdi acknowledged. But Monteverdi seems to have been the first man to point out the need to make music the servant of the words, and to make this a distinctive feature of the new style which was to play such an important part in the development of opera. The novelty of the idea even later made it necessary for Saint Evremond to emphasize, as something out of the ordinary in France, that 'the music must be made for the words, rather than the words for the music'.[2] Yet the emphasis did not remain securely balanced with the poet as the dominating figure: during the first quarter of the eighteenth century the relationship tended to alter its balance. There was a tendency to see the music not as a pointer to the full meaning of the text but as some greater force that could take the words and absorb them into some more potent solution: 'd'appliquer aux paroles des tons si proportionnés, que la Poésie étant confondue et revivant dans la Musique: celle-ci porte jusqu'au fond du cœur de l'auditeur le sentiment de tout ce que le Chanteur dit.'[3]

[1] Alfred Einstein, *The Italian Madrigal*, p. 494.

[2] *The letters of Saint Evremond*, ed. John Hayward, London, 1930, p. 210, letter 'To the Duke of Buckingham upon operas', 1678.

[3] Jacques Bonnet and Pierre Bourdelot, *Histoire de la Musique et ses effets*, Amsterdam, 1725, vol. ii, p. 163.

Hence it would seem that music was considered to be endowed with almost chemical powers into which the words, like sugar, dissolved. But the ancient balance could be upset even more. In fact, the Italian critic Muratori was of the opinion that the operas of his own day were a complete reversal of the art as the early masters saw it. 'At one time', he writes, 'music was the servant and waited on the poetry, now the poetry is the servant of the music.'[1] In fact, the high esteem in which the eighteenth century held Metastasio was due to the fact that his verses were exempt from such criticism: they did not drown the music but ruled, lightly, like a mistress, as his latest biographer informs us in an interesting chapter on contemporary criticism.[2] Gluck is often held up as the reformer of the opera who brought back the balance by restoring to poetry her rightful place and, in consequence, his reforms have occupied a larger proportion of space in histories of music than has the performance of his music in public opera-houses. Yet, although his genius gave new power to the opera, the reforms, of which he is held as the author, were simply the application of theories held in common with the *avant-garde* musical world of the day; theories that had been discussed for some years. The group of enthusiasts in Vienna, Count Durazzo, the ballet master Angiolini, Guadagni the original Orfeo, and Gluck himself were largely the advocates of a style urged by Metastasio throughout his life. Their debt to him has formal expression in Calzabigi's preface to the works in the edition of 1755. The view which holds Metastasio in contempt for exalting the musician above the poet owes its prevalence largely to Burney's description of the two camps in Vienna in his *Musical Tour*;[3] he speaks of the Metastasian party whose composer was Hasse, and the new school of Calzabigi and Gluck, from which it would appear that the two camps were mutually exclusive to each other. The contrary becomes obvious from a perusal of Burney's own translation of Metastasio's letters. Wagner, equally mistaken, takes the view that he 'remained always the well-disciplined and most pliable servant of the musician'.[4]

Roughly speaking, then, the hundred-odd years from 1637 can show

---

[1] Lodovico Muratori, *Della Perfetta Poesia Italiana*, Venice, 1730, vol. ii, p. 34: 'e laddove la Musica una volta era serva, e ministra di lei, ora la Poesia è serva della Musica.'

[2] Luigi Russo, *Metastasio*, 3rd. ed., Bari, 1945, p. 195: 'La poesia non sarà annegata nella musica, ma dominerà da padrona—clemente, è vero—sulla musica.'

[3] Charles Burney, *The Present State of Music in Germany*, London, 1773, vol. i, pp. 232-3.

[4] Richard Wagner, *Opera and Drama*, tr. Edwin Evans, sen., vol. i, p. 29.

the relationship between poet and musician completing a circle. During the early decades of public opera it would appear that the onus of the production depended on the poet. The formalities of publication were his responsibility; he chose the patron to whom the play was to be dedicated; he derived an income from the sale of the libretto. And all that remained to testify to a performance was often the duodecimo, paper-bound book with the print wax-stained from the little candle, by the light of which the story was followed in the theatre. The music, either in parts or score, was never printed, irrespective of the success of the work. For example, the libretto of one of Cesti's most renowned operas, *La Dori*,[1] performed, according to Loewenberg, in most of the important centres of Italy and Austria within the twenty years of its first appearance in Florence in 1661, went into three editions in Venice during 1663, 1666, and 1667. Yet the preface to the final edition, whilst expressing satisfaction that the work had been universally acclaimed, explains that great difficulty had been experienced in finding the original music, in editing it, and bringing the parts from one theatre to another; for it was produced by two different companies within the space of a year.[2] Clearly, then, the poet had a far larger public for the spread of his work than the composer, whose score was allowed to moulder in some lumber-room of the theatre.

In spite of the predominant position of the poet, there seems to have been some attempt at a genuine collaboration. Monteverdi held out strongly for the rights of musicians against librettists as his letters to the Secretary of the Duke of Mantua, Count Striggio, indicate. He was able to persuade the poet that not every situation is capable of musical interpretation. Count Badovero, one of the librettists of his last operas, was alive to the need of adapting his versification and language to suit the peculiar requirements of an opera. Although his own works lack inspiration, it is significant that he realized that the problem existed.[3] And there are rare occasions where an opera was considered the work as much of the musician as the poet. Cesti and Apolloni were hailed as the twin parents of *Argia*.[4] If this joint creative

---

[1] For parts of this opera cf. vol. xii of *Publikationen der Gesellschaft für Musikforschung*.

[2] Ecco la Dori acclamata e richiesta universalmente da ognuno. Si è incontrato molta difficultà nel ritrovare l'originale della musica, come nell' aggiustarlo e nel trasportare le parti.

[3] *Argomento et Scenario* for *Le Nozze d'Enea con Lavinia*.

[4] *L'Argia*. Drama per musica da rappresentarsi nel Teatro à San Salvatore, 1669: 'Basta che io ti dinoti esser ella figlia di quei genitori de' quali applaudesti alla Dori.'

effort was seldom recognized, some tribute was generally paid to the composer in the preface to the libretto, either by name or by some highly complimentary phrase such as 'il miracolo della musica' or 'l'Anfione di nostro giorno'. But the fact that librettos were set by so many composers led to the latter more general designation being preferred.

The predominance of the librettist in the partnership is partly due to the form of the poetry. When the libretto was written largely to suit the declamatory style of recitative the words had a significance which they would lose in an aria, designed for the convenience of the musician so that he could alter word order and repeat lines as his musical invention demanded.

As the love for arias grew the audience turned more and more to the composer, and with him the singer, as the principal instruments for their pleasure. In the first two impressions of Aureli's *Helena rapita da Paride*[1] of 1677 the author is not mentioned, whilst the composer's name is given in both. Sonneck[2] shows the alteration in arias from one edition to the other, and also gives details of a third performance in 1687,[3] in which a second composer, Francesco Navarra, not only composed several additional arias for this revival of Freschi's opera, but also changed some of the latter's arias 'per agiustarsi all' abilità de musici che le cantano'. A previous instance of deliberate interpolation comes from Corradi's *Germanico sul Reno*, in which violin solos are especially introduced, one of which seems to have been played because of demand from the public.[4]

The nature of the audience changed during the last quarter of the century. Venice became the centre of a cosmopolitan society in music[5] and the arts. For example, a director of the Roman Academy suggested that students would gain little from study there but should visit Venice and other towns in Lombardy.[6] It is possible that the increase in arias was due partly to the demands of this class of audience anxious to hear examples of the new art of opera.

---

[1] *Helena rapita da Paride*. Drama per musica nel Teatro Novissimo di S. Anbelo. Text, Aureli; music, Domenico Freschi.   [2] Oscar Sonneck, op. cit., p. 589.

[3] *Helena rapita da Paride*. Drama per musica nel Teatro Zane à S. Moisè di Aurelio Aureli. Seconda impressione, Venice, 1687.

[4] *Germanico sul Reno*. Drama per musica da rappresentarsi nel Famosissimo Teatro Vendramino di San Salvatore. Venice, 1676. Text, G. C. Corradi; music, Giò. Legrenzi.

[5] Egon Wellesz, *Zwei Studien zur Geschichte der Oper im XVII. Jahrh.* SIMG, xv, pp. 125.

[6] Nikolaus Pevsner, *Academies of Art past and present*, Cambridge, 1940, p. 105.

However, it would be wrong to conclude that an interest in the composer and singer implied an interest in and appreciation of music itself. The quality of the scores rather declines as the composers have to yield to the claims of virtuoso singers. An opera, originally commissioned from Cesti, *Il Genserico* is one of the earliest in which the claims of the singers are recognized. In the libretto the printer has added the additional arias with a note to the effect that they have been introduced to please the cast.[1] The new designation of melodrama may be itself significant of the shift of emphasis on to the singers. These additional arias are seldom included in the manuscript scores since they are the result of impromptu composition at rehearsals. But the librettos give valuable information on the subject. And it is clear that the singer ruled supreme. Their powers were such that the lines in librettos were altered so that each singer could take a quatrain where originally the text was a dialogue. These quatrains could then be set as arias by the composer. An example of such treatment is to be found in the two settings of Minato's *Scipione Africano*,[2] the first to Cavalli's music and the second[3] textually adapted by Tebaldo Fattorini and musically by Bonaventura Viviani. The second edition informs the reader that new canzoni have been included according to the modern habit.

	1664 Edition		*1678 Edition*
Pol:	Bellezza sdegnosa	*Pol:*	Bellezza sdegnosa
	Gradirmi non può.		Gradirmi non può
Lucc:	Sembianza vezzosa		Sembianza vezzosa
	Giamai gradirò.		Io sempre amerò.
Pol:	M'invita e diletta	*Lucc:*	Mi piace, e m'alletta
	Piacevole Amor.		Sol rigido Amor.
Lucc:	Mi piace, m'alletta		M'invita, e diletta
	Superbo vigor.		Superbo rigor.

The taste for arias is fully recognized in Cesti's *Argia*; the prologue to this opera, found in the libretto but not in the manuscript score

[1] *Il Genserico.* Melodrama da rappresentarsi nel Famoso Teatro Grimano à SS. Giò. e Paolo. Venice, 1669. Text, Nic. Beregen N.V.; music, M. A. Cesti, finished by Gio. Dom. Partenio. 'E per far compeggiar maggiormente la virtù de i Cantanti sono stati mutati molti Versi, onde per sodisfare alla curiosità di chi legge hò voluto imprimarli sopra questo foglio con l'ordine, che segue.'

[2] *Scipione Africano.* Drama per musica nel Teatro à SS. Giò. e Paolo, Venice, 1664.

[3] *Scipione Africano.* Drama per musica nel famoso Teatro Grimani à SS. Giò. e Paolo, Venice, 1678. 'Maggiormente al genio corrente è stato necessario di ridurlo a qualche brevità, ed accrescerlo nelle canzoni.'

in the Marciana library, represents the Muses who take down from the shelves of the room in which they stand different opera books and sing arias from them. The poet Aureli admits in the preface to *Claudio Cesare*[1] (1672) that the plot has had to be considerably simplified in order to include many arias within the natural length of an opera. In the score there are sixty-six arias. Aureli does mention the composer Boretti in his preface. But, clearly, both are under compulsion from singer and public, writing for no other reason than to provide that entertainment required by popular taste. Such was the craze for arias that additional songs, by authors other than the poet, were inserted into the librettos. The preface to Stanzzini's *Arsinoe*[2] explains these extra verses, and again echoes the complaint against contemporary taste. Even a composer with a European reputation such as Cesti could not be certain that his works after his death would remain unaltered, for no producer would dare include in a new production music that the audience might know.[3]

Although in one sense composers of late-seventeenth-century operas sacrificed much of the dramatic power of the old masters by larding scores too richly with arias, the habit of incorporating solo songs into dramatic entertainment is an interesting factor in the development of opera itself. Both the monodic frottole and the later madrigals have

[1] *Claudio Cesare*. Drama per musica nel Teatro Vendramino à San Salvatore. Venice, 1672. Text, A. Aureli; music, G. A. Boretti: 'ti presento il mio Claudio ricco più di canzoni, e d'ariette, che d'accidenti. Basti il dire, che sia Drama per Musica. Che si può fare? s'oggi dì i capricci di Venezia cosi la vogliono, io procuro d'incontrar il lor gusto. . . . Doppo stampata, e provata l'Opera sovra la Scena s'hà stimato bene d'abbreviarla in varie parti superflue; onde sei pregato a trascorrer benignamente con l'occhio alquanti versi, e qualche Scene, che per maggior brevità si tralasciano, non havendosi potuto apportarli per esser la stampata già fatta. Qui sotto leggerai anco trè ariette mutate, il tutto fatto à solo fine di cantar solo quello, che si vede, che possa maggiormente dilettar gl'Uditori. Compatisce le difficoltà ch' oggidì provano li comipositori nel poter sodisfare non solo à tanti capricci bizarri di questa Città; ma anco à gl'humori stravaganti de' Signori Musici recitanti.'

[2] *Arsinoe*. Drama per Musica. Da recitarsi nel Teatro di S. Angelo, Venice, 1677. Text, Stanzzini: music, Franceschini.

[3] *La Schiava Fortunata*. Drama per Musica da rappresentare nel Portentoso Teatro Zane à San Moisè. Venice, 1674. Text, G. A. Moniglia; music, M. A. Ziani: 'Elegata nell' Oro finissimo di Musichali Note del Sign. Caval. Cesti, si lasciò persuadere, doppo una Pomposa Mostra all' Invitte Pupille dell' Aquila Austriaca farne altresi delitiosa comparsa nel Teatro Zane à S. Moisè; Dove, prima di lasciarsi vedere, benche di perfettissima struttura, ma nell' ordine superficiale manchevole, fù di nuovo ritoccata [by G. C. Corradi] d'Ariette, Introduttione, Intermedii, e qualche piccola Scena, che, smaltata con natural bizzaria dall' Armonico Stile del Sig. Marc Antonio Ziani, la ridusse in figura del Moderno universal compiacciamento, e fece maggiormente spiccare il suo antico pretioso valore.'

important contributions to make in this connexion. The *Orfeo* by Poliziano has been acclaimed as the fountain of modern opera. It was written to celebrate the entry of Cardinal Francesco Gonzaga into Mantua in 1471 or 1472 and seems to have been a mixture of declamation and song. But Isaac and Poliziano collaborated in a lament to mark the death of Lorenzo il Magnifico in Florence so that monody was an established custom at the time. Festivities that demanded acting and singing gave pleasure in the northern Italian towns, particularly Florence, where Isaac had been so successful in reviving the *canti carnascialeschi* in which a certain amount of acting was incorporated into the four-part musical compositions. But Urbino, Mantua, and Ferrara were the great centres of musical activity during the early part of the sixteenth century. Castiglione, the author of *Il Libro del Cortegiano* (1528), combined with Francesco Gonzaga to produce at Urbino in 1508 an eclogue, *Tirsi*, in which canzonette were interspersed with passages of declamation.[1] And at Ferrara we have a clear reference to the operatic ideal by the middle of the century. The tragedy *Orbecche*[2] (1541) by Cinzio was produced there in a private house with music and scenery, the music being composed by Alfonso della Viola. His music for *Il Sacrificio* by Beccari, also produced in Ferrara thirteen years later, contains a very early extant piece of dramatic monody[3] for the priest of Pan sung by his brother, 'rappresentò il Sacerdote con la lira M. Andrea suo fratello'. There may be a resemblance between this type of play with songs to lute accompaniment and the Venetian stage productions, described by Solerti[4] as dating from 1571, that celebrate the victory at Lepanto and continue into the first decade of the new century. These plays were on various subjects, one being based on a historical plot, *Il Trionfo di Scipione in Cartagena* (1595), that anticipates the later Venetian type. They were performed four times a year, for the feasts of St. Stephen, St. Mark, the Ascension, and St. Vito. The composers of the music are not always known, although Claudio Merulo set one in honour of the visit of Henry III to Venice in 1574 on his way from Poland to Paris. It was evidently composed

[1] Giosuè Carducci, *Su Ludovico Ariosto e Torquato Tasso*, Bologna, 1905, p. 383.

[2] Angelo Solerti, *Gli albori del melodramma*, 1904, vol. i, intr., p. 6: 'La rappresentò Messer Sebastiano Clarignano da Montefalco. Fece la Musica Mess. Alfonso della Viola. Fu l'Architetto et il Dipintore della scena Messer Girolamo Carpi da Ferrara.'   [3] Ibid., vol. i, pp. 1–6.

[4] Angelo Solerti, 'Le Rappresentazioni musicali di Venezia, 1571 al 1605', *R.M.I.*, vol. ix, 1902, pp. 503 sqq.

throughout, sometimes for chorus and sometimes for solo. The cast lists musicians with lutes. And the songs may have resembled the earlier monodies or dramatic dialogues of Ruffo that Einstein can imagine 'within the framework of a pastoral or even of a genuine tragedy'.[1] This composer was employed by the earliest of the Italian musical academies, the *Accademia Filarmonica* at Verona, that flourished from the mid-century; there were many links between its members and Venice. In view of the popularity of stage performances it is not surprising to find stage properties and scenery amongst their possessions in an inventory of 1585.[2]

The whole development of the madrigal in Italy, from the 'frottole' for solo voice and lute accompaniment which the earlier songs must have resembled to the pseudo-monody of the penultimate chapter in Einstein's *Italian Madrigals*, leads us more and more to conclude that the aria *per se* had a far older place in musical literature than the operas, cantatas, and collections of solo songs of the seventeenth century. And, although a book of this nature cannot deal with such a wide subject, it is worth digressing shortly in discussing the aria and the libretto in order to hint that the poets and composers with whom we are dealing were following a tradition when they added the arias to the scenes of their operas. It cannot be a coincidence, for instance, that the great writers of the expressive madrigals, Cipriano da Rore and Giaches de Wert, 'one of the real intermediaries between Rore and Monteverdi',[3] who was commissioned to write the intermezzos for a 'commedia' for Alfonso I Gonzaga in a new theatre in 1568, should choose poems such as *Orlando furioso* (1516) or the *Gerusalemme liberata* (1581), scenes from which were to form the basis for so many later plots or that their settings are capable of monodic interpretation[4] and written, although in five parts, in a real 'stile recitativo'.[5] Wert is in fact one of the important pre-aria aria composers. From a setting of verses from the sixteenth canto of the *Gerusalemme liberata* in his eighth book, Einstein considers him as 'standing at the beginning of the series that ends with Gluck's *Armide*, indeed, with Wagner's *Tannhäuser*'.[6] He seems,

[1] Alfred Einstein, *The Italian Madrigal*, p. 468.
[2] Giuseppe Turrini, *L'Accademia Filarmonica di Verona*, Verona, 1941, p. 186: 'Una scena comica di tela sopra i telari, con proscenio, et cielo di sopra, in piedi piantata.'
[3] Alfred Einstein, op. cit., p. 512.
[4] Ibid., vol. iii, No 68. *Dunque basciar si belle e dolce labbia*, Ariosto, Wert.
[5] Ibid., vol. iii, No. 69. *Giunto a la tomba ove al suo spirito vivo*, Tasso, Wert. [6] Ibid., pp. 569–70.

at times, to be conscious even of the distinction between recitative and aria. Petrarch, too, is another poet who attracted the expressive modern composers of the mid- and late-sixteenth century. And one is reminded of the comparison drawn by Russo between Petrarch and Metastasio, as the affecting poet *par excellence* of aria verse.[1] In later composers, the *Camerata Bardi* and their school, it is of course easy to see the sources for many later arias. Yet the earlier attempts in which some form of song was mixed with drama, song that itself was intended to produce a similar effect in later arias through its powers of expression, show how well the ground had been prepared for the later poets and composers.

A similar tradition can be traced in the sources of the plots. Yet here, just as many of the composers of monodies were *oltramontani*, the models for the librettists were the works of Spanish dramatists. For, even in those parts of Italy not actually ruled by Spain, the influence of its literary forces was felt. In Venice the most important literary body, the *Accademia degli Incogniti* (1630), was founded by Gian Francesco Loredan, a man renowned for his translations from the Spanish.[2] The melodramatic plot, so suitable for opera librettos, was widespread in the many novels which flooded into Italy during the century. '*I romances* correvano per l'Italia',[3] writes Croce. Plays, too, were based on Spanish models. It is significant that Jacopo Cicognini, the father of a celebrated librettist Giancinto Andrea Cicognini, was probably the first Italian to write a play on the Don Giovanni legend, the *Convitato di Pietra*, round about 1653.[4] The Italian version is remarkable for the introduction of comic scenes, a notable development in the librettos and scores of Venetian operas. Belloni quotes a letter to Jacopa Cicognini from Lope De Vega in which he urged him to write in the new way and not to follow the old rules for the Unities.[5] Cicognini refers to this advice in the preface to a play *Il trionfo di David* (1633). And it is interesting to find that the best of the early Venetian librettists should mention the custom in the preface to *La Didone* (1641) set by Cavalli. Gio. Francesco Busenello explains that the plot is not written according to the ancient rules, but follows

[1] Luigi Russo, *Metastasio*, Bari, 1945, p. 90: 'fratello minore del sognante Petrarca.'
[2] Benedetto Croce, *Nuovi Saggi sulla Letteratura Italiana del Seicento*, Bari, 1949, pp. 235–9.
[3] Ibid., p. 237.
[4] Antonio Belloni, *Storia Letteraria d'Italia, Il Seicento*, Milan, 1943, p. 357.
[5] Ibid., p. 354.

Spanish tradition by measuring time in years instead of hours.[1] In fact, the unities are preserved or not according to the wishes of the poet. But in general the antecedents of the action are explained to the audience in a note in the text. And the opera itself is the dénouement of a complicated set of circumstances from which a happy ending must be resolved. The action therefore seldom has need to break the unity of time.

Although Spanish influence is manifest, opera plots had indigenous roots of their own. The drama of *Torresmondo* by Tasso, which ran to eleven editions within five months of publication[2] in 1587, is an obvious source for the type of plot in which substitutions, mistaken identities, and last-minute identifications by old servants to prevent disasterous marriages, abound. *L'Argia*,[3] a representative libretto, combines the erotic interest of a Tasso poem with the *capa y espada* melodramatic incident of a Spanish story in which excitement and buffoonery can be found. The antecedents of the situation are explained in the preface; Lucimoro and Dorisbe are brother and sister, Cyprian princes. Lucimoro is captured as a child by pirates, and adopted as son by the king of Thrace with the name of Selino. Sent off as a young man to travel, he falls in love with a princess of Negroponte, Argia, whom he leaves with child, continuing his tour with a visit to Cyprus. Argia, wishing to find her betrayer, decides to follow him there, and disguises herself as a man, Laurindo. Her brother Feraspe decides to visit Cyprus as well, drawn by the famous beauty of Dorisbe and less strongly by the need to recover his sister. The opera opens, after a sinfonia in five parts, with his party landing on the island; a chorus gives the theme of the plot, singing:

> Naviganti à riva, à riva
> Già risplende in Ciel l'Aurora,
> Quest' è Cipro, e qui s'adora
> Delle Dee la più lasciva.
> Naviganti à riva, à riva.

Feraspe meets Laurindo (Argia) of whom he inquires the way to court. She does not disclose her identity. Selino (Lucimoro) falls in love with

---

[1] 'Quest' Opera sente delle opinioni moderne. Non è fatta al prescritto delle Antiche regole; ma all' usanza Spagnola rappresenta gl'anni, e non le hore.'

[2] Giosuè Carducci, op. cit., p. 491.

[3] *L'Argia*. Drama per musica da rappresentarsi nel Teatro à San Salvatore, Venice, 1669. Text, A. Apolloni; music, A. Cesti.

Dorisbe and Argia (Laurindo), hearing of it, prepares to kill herself. Laurindo is discovered lying on the ground by a courtesan, kept by the king of Cyprus, Atamante. She makes love to the disguised princess who violently repulses her advances in a comic scene. The act ends with a dance of slaves and a song by Aleco the eunuch, a buffo character. The second act is introduced by some florid singing from the goddess Venere as an indication of the main element in the act. Feraspe procures an audience from Dorisbe and declares his love at once. Later Laurindo is about to disclose her true identity to Selino, until he tells her of his love for Dorisbe, whereupon she decided furiously that he must die, not her. There is a double drama for the audience, since Argia's anger is for his infidelity to her, sufficient reason for his death in her eyes, whereas, for the audience, he is now guilty of an incestuous love. However, in spite of the elements of tragedy in the plot, reminiscent of *Torresmondo*, it seems probable that the audience were more interested by the intrigue and the parody of court behaviour for a buffo scene between the old nurse and the court jester allows them to imitate the love-making of their betters. The act ends with a 'ballo di Fantasmi'. Act III opens with Laurindo (Argia) in prison after her discovery by the king in the garden with Dorisbe, also imprisoned, and Selino, who is threatened with banishment. His baby and Osmano, who alone knows both the secret of its birth and the real parentage of its father, appear above the dungeon. The baby, precociously begs to be allowed to die with its mother. The reason for the imprisonment is that the king had thought Laurindo's behaviour improper towards his daughter. However, her intentions in fact had been to entice Selino out alone in order to kill him. She is released through the good offices of the courtesan, to whom she gives a promise of her affections. However, as she is being released, there is a great call to arms at court. This appears to convince her of Selino's murder. In fact it is the summons for a joust in which Feraspe comes to challenge Atamante to prove his accusations against Dorisbe. At the last moment Laurindo enters as a champion on Atamante's behalf. Laurindo accuses Selino and Dorisbe of misconduct; they are condemned to drink poison by the king. But, as they are about to drink, Laurindo discloses herself as Argia, which places Selino in an even more awkward situation. At this moment Osman, a comparatively unimportant character to date, is discovered. He is, in fact, the *deus ex machina* of the story, a convenience without which the plot could not be satisfactorily explained. He was Selino's tutor, and was captured by the pirates with him. He eventually became a hermit at Negroponte, and was given care of Argia's child, the son, as chance would have it, of his own pupil Lucimoro, as we know. The opera can then end abruptly with the engagement of Dorisbe to Feraspe, and the legitimizing of the old *liaison* between Argia and Lucimoro.

Such a plot lacks no excitement from the point of view of action, but is devoid of any real interest as far as the study of character is concerned. It is typical of the majority of such stories. The audience was concerned more with the recognition scenes, and the *double entendre* for which the disguises provide so many opportunities, and which naturally prevent the portrayal of a true character-study. To meet the requirements of the singers, it was incumbent on the poet to provide as many occasions as possible for the main characters to leave the stage in order that the composer could give them an aria, for such was the custom. The plot thus suffers from a certain instability and lack of continuity.

The historical plots, of which Busenello's *L'Incoronatione di Poppea* is the first, followed a similar plan to that illustrated by *L'Argia*. There was no attempt to stick closely to the original as far as the dénouement was concerned, although the events leading up to it were authentic. There was one obligation, however, that the poet had to fulfil. Care was taken to keep the plot within the bounds of probability as recognized by contemporary critics.[1] The sources for such plots were more often medieval than classical, events from the histories of hellenistic authors.

Although the more popular plots were woven around historical or purely imaginary melodramatic stories, the old type of *favola pastorale*, deriving from the classical eclogue through the academies of the renaissance, still had some following; but the final result in a libretto is a bastard child. Tasso's *Aminta*, for example, is far removed from such librettos as Persiani's *Le Nozze di Teti e di Peleo*,[2] in which the pastoral landscape is filled with figures from classical mythology, disporting themselves as in some picture by Rubens. The prologue

---

[1] *Scipione Africano*. Drama per musica nel Teatro à SS. Giò. e Paolo, Venice, 1664. Text, Minato; music, Cavalli: 'Sopra questi fatti Historici si fita l'intreccio di questo Drama circondandoli delli seguenti verisimili.'

[2] *Le Nozze di Teti e di Peleo*. Dramma recitato nel Teatro di San Cassiano di Venezia. Venice, 1639. Text, Orazio Persiani; music, Cavalli.

to the opera is sung in recitative by *la Fama* and *il Tempo*. Act I opens
with the well-known 'concilio infernale' in which the gods work out
the fate of the principal characters, and the scene ends with a chorus
of hunters. The main plot is based on the story of Teti and her rival
lovers Peleo and Tritone. We are introduced to Teti and Peleo in
Scene 3. But Tritone in Scene 4 enters with followers, who spoil the
love-making by attacking Peleo. The stage alters and the gods are
shown again in council. Giove, who had desired Teti, is told that a
child of his will be greater than he. This news decides him to plot the
union of Peleo with Teti. The scene returns once more to the earth
where Peleo, Meleagro, and knights rejoice in their victory over the
Tritons; but Peleo laments the disappearance of Teti. Two gods
descend to proclaim Giove's will in a scene of musical interest, treated
as a unity in which the sung phrases of the two gods and Peleo are
separated by the repetition of a little three-bar *ciacconia*. The messen-
gers leave the stage, and Tritone reappears followed by Teti whom he
attempts to carry away. However, this is prevented by nymphs. And
the act ends with a short chorus followed by an instrumental piece.
In Act II we have to imagine that Peleo has disappeared. Teti and
Peleo's friend Meleagro lament him as dead; she leaves the stage. But
he has been sleeping, unnoticed by them, in a corner: he himself
explains to Meleagro that he had thought that Teti had been carried
off in the fight of the previous Act. Persiani now brings in a new character, Discordia. She and two gods arise from the Inferno to visit Peleo,
and are joined later by Chirone and Centaur. Centaur is made Peleo's
confidant, and is asked both to find Teti, and to calm a love-sick soul
with sweet music. The effect is magical, for Teti, hearing the sounds,
enters to investigate, sees Peleo, and at first imagines the form to be
his ghost, but upon seeing her mistake joins him in a duet of joy followed by a dance of centaurs. The gods enter and a great feast is prepared for the happy couple. A little diversion is introduced by Giove,
who notices the absence of Bacchus. However, he soon enters with a
train of Bacchanals who initiate a chorus, taken up by the whole company in praise of wine. But, at this point, Persiani introduces a new
element to provide scope for a third act. Discordia enters with the
apple, and the judgement follows in which Juno receives the prize from
Peleo. A further chorus of joy ends the act. The third act is extremely
complicated. Discordia has turned against Peleo and Teti as the use

of the apple must have implied in Act II. Pluto, the enemy of true love, has ordered Discordia to impersonate Meleagro. In this disguise she insinuates to Peleo that Teti is unfaithful to him and, to prove her point, brings him to the spot at which Teti is lamenting to herself Peleo's lack of chivalry in the previous Act, when he did not award her the golden apple. The pair enter as she exclaims, 'O Peleo, troppo villano!' which convinces Peleo of her treachery. But Discordia wishes to double the proof. She leaves Peleo hidden and re-enters the stage dressed as Nereo, who, unknown to Peleo, is father to Teti. He caresses his daughter. Peleo imagines that he must be a lover, and, furious, leaves the stage. Discordia, still disguised, argues with Teti that Peleo is not in love with her at all, and desires marriage for convenience only. The object of his affections is a nymph, Margellina. She carries Teti off to witness Peleo's perfidy and leads her to a concealed place. Meanwhile, having left her, she disguises herself as the nymph, and leads Peleo on to the stage. He confides to her his grief. Teti, seeing them so deep in a lovers' conversation, despairingly decides to kill herself. The main plot is now left and the scene changes to the woods of Ida. The mythological story of the golden apple is acted and Paris awards the apple to Venus. A dance of 'amoretti' follows, and the scene returns to the Lido where Discordia is exulting at the success of her schemes. She flies up to heaven to continue to make mischief amongst the gods. Meanwhile Peleo enters intending to accuse Teti of unfaithfulness and is met by a knight (Teti in disguise) who challenges him to a duel. But the incompatible Himeneo and Discordia descend in mutual rage; Discordia is dispatched to the kingdom of Pluto whilst Himeneo unites the lovers. A finale declaring the theme that virtue has its own reward finishes the plot.

The characteristic of these pastorals is a combination of dance and song with a loosely connected and therefore complicated plot running throughout, which allows of subsidiary plots suitable for musical settings of a fairly elaborate nature. However, the Venetian habit of depending more upon dramatic episodes for the chief characters than ensemble scenes was not favourable for such treatment. In fact, they are not to be found in Venice after the first few years of performances in public opera-houses, at least until the cosmopolitan influence of Vienna and Paris reacted upon taste there. Such operas as Cesti's *Pomo d'oro* (1668) were foreign to the Venetian tradition. The Marciana has scores for two mythological plots,[1] and Faustini's *Egisto*[2] is a modified example that was popular throughout Italy. And plots based on Marino's *La Catena d'Adone*[3] are used from time to time through the century. And, of course, the story of *Orfeo*, in many versions, is a never-failing source for musical inspiration. But these no longer resemble the old pastoral or satiric drama but take on the characteristics of the modern plots, the characters differing from the princes and princesses in history only by name.

The cause of such a decline in popularity is certainly due to the principle of the *veresimile*. The historical plots or romances were more convincing than the phantasy of mythology. For it was only towards the end of the century through the studies of men like Vico that the ancient myths were felt to possess a deeper significance. The early operatic public enjoyed stories for the possibilities they offered to the machine-maker. But once the stages were equipped with means that enabled the producer to incorporate mechanical devices, other than flights of gods, then the plots with more immediate appeal were held in greater esteem, particularly since they were available in the Spanish novels so highly considered in contemporary literary circles.

---

[1] *Gli Amori d'Apollo e di Dafne* di Francesco Busenello. Rappresentati in musica nel Teatro di S. Cassiano, Venice, 1640. Music, Cavalli. *Amore inamorato*. Favola da Rappresentarsi in musica nel Teatro di S. Moisè, Venice, 1642. Text, G. B. Fusconi; music, Cavalli.

[2] Alfred Loewenberg, *Annals of Opera*, Cambridge, 1943, p. 12.

[3] Antonio Belloni, op. cit., pp. 416–17.

The Place of Opera in the Aesthetics of the Seventeenth Century

The principle of art during the seventeenth century was imitation: imitation of nature, a phrase which had recurred at an early date in books on painting and literature in the previous century, but had not been introduced into discussions on the aesthetics of music much before the time of Monteverdi.[1] The new cosmology of the sixteenth century in which matter could be distinguished on a quantitative basis, had given rise to a more exact study of the physical world in which it was considered that all objects differed solely in structure. The common basis of all matter therefore made analogy a favourite means of expression. The relationship between words and music took on a new significance. Music had to express to the full the meaning of the text and to produce an emotional reaction in the audience, the kind of reaction at which the *seconda pratica* of Monteverdi aimed, and which, at the time, was startling in its novelty. Monteverdi emphasized his intentions to 'make the words the mistress of the harmony and not the servant' and thus showed his compatriots the only method of composition suitable for *musica rappresentativa* or theatrical music.

The problems involved in the imitation of nature in a medium such as opera are perhaps more complicated than in any other art. The term 'nature' itself requires a stricter definition than it would when considered as a poetic image or as a carefully drawn or modelled representation of the human form. The opera loosens a painting from the moment in time, gives life to the particular incident represented in the complicated existence of the subject. It provides, too, all the *nuances* of timbre both instrumental (although the seventeenth century hardly exploited the orchestra) and the voice, which could convey shades of meaning, evoke, through the powers of harmony and melody, the remembrance of other situations, and give new twists to character outside the scope of drama. The immediate question was to define the

[1] Alfred Einstein, *The Italian Madrigal*, p. 321.

scope of the new art. The generally accepted aims for art as a whole were to please and to instruct, 'religion and good manners only excepted';[1] art must not transgress against the tested standards of the age, must instruct yet not offend. Such a view is proof against the charge of smugness since, by setting up as an example the best in nature, the individual shortcomings of the audience were made doubly shocking. Conscience was stirred and the affections or passions moved.

By welding music to drama new problems are presented which had not arisen when music had been attached to drama. Should music literally imitate the sound of nature; should it create in the listener an emotional response corresponding to the general situation presented to him in each opera, or should it enhance word by word the poetry of the text. It could, of course, do all three. Representational music, largely dependent on instruments, became a characteristic of French opera, with its storm-scenes, battles, and various subjects easily lending themselves to literal imitation. But Italian opera in the early days, through the developing relationship between aria and recitative, concentrated both on expressing the general mood as well as the particular word. The question for both composers and poets was to decide what subjects and words were best expressed in music. The preface to Monteverdi's *Madrigali guerrieri ed amorosi* (1638) deals with this problem of imitation. 'To obtain a better proof', he says, 'I took the divine Tasso, as a poet who expresses with the greatest propriety and naturalness the qualities which he wishes to describe, and selected his description of the combat of Tancred and Clorinda as an opportunity of describing in music contrary passions, namely warfare, entreaty and death',[2] thus enlarging the number of passions capable of musical imitation.

This problem of imitation had only lately begun to interest musicians in any wide sense. The music of the *prima pratica* had marked out various works which lent themselves to literal interpretation. But the wider implications of an imitation of nature had scarcely entered into musical aesthetics, and were still not entirely understood in the great period of operatic production in Venice.

Even the general meaning of the term nature, in the later seventeenth-century interpretation, requires a little clarification. Were

[1] John Dryden, dedication of *Examen Poeticum*, 1693, ed. W. P. Ker, Oxford, 1900, vol. ii, p. 7.
[2] Translation in Oliver Strunk, *Source Readings in Music History*, New York, 1950, pp. 413–15.

librettists to consider it, for example, to imply a primeval state un-
affected by civilization, or did it mean the perfected state towards
which nature was striving. Had the opera plot to represent what is, or
has been, or what ought to be. For example, Dryden considered that
poetry and painting 'are not only true imitations of nature, but of the
best nature, of that which is wrought up to a nobler pitch'.[1] Such
opinions affected the trend of thought of the day and had an important
bearing on the librettos. Dryden was himself conversant with Italian
practice, partly through its influence on the French taste, the model
for the court life in London, and partly through direct Italian sources,
and can accordingly illuminate the subject. It is significant, for
example, that scenario, a word for which Italian dictionaries do not
give instances earlier than the late seventeenth century, was first
adapted in English as 'scenery' by Dryden.[2] And he bases the argument
in *A Parallel of Poetry and Painting* upon points made by Bellori in his
Vite de' Pittori (1672). He was familiar, too, with the works of Mascardi.[3]
In fact, his dramatic intentions illustrate the lines upon which Italian
thought ran. Professor Mario Praz says that 'Scaramouch' became
popular in England after the clever impersonation of the part by
Tiberio Fiurelli, who took his company of Italian players to London
in 1673.[4] Dryden himself mentions that 'we see the daily examples of
them [the commedia dell' arte impromptu performances] in the Italian
farces of Harlequin and Scaramucha'.[5] And, with reference to D'Ave-
nant's *Siege of Rhodes*, he judges that the 'original of this musick, and
of the Scenes which adorn'd his work, he had from the Italian Opera's'.[6]
This essay was written in the year previous to Fiurelli's visit and it
seems reasonable to suppose that they would have talked of the new
art of the opera. The list, too, of travellers who must have had first-
hand knowledge of continental opinion is long. Amongst the Englishmen who had a practical experience of opera abroad, besides the exiled
court, it is worth mentioning the singer Stafford who came from Rome
to Paris in 1654 with Caproli to perform in *Le Nozze di Peleo e di Teti*.[7]

[1] John Dryden, *A Parallel of Poetry and Painting*, 1695, ed. W. P. Ker, vol. ii, p. 137.

[2] Mario Praz, 'The Italian element in English', *Essays and Studies*, English Association, vol. xv,
p. 45. Oxford, 1929.

[3] John Dryden, *A Discourse concerning the Original and Progress of Satire*, 1693, ed. W. P. Ker,
vol. ii, p. 103.   [4] Mario Praz, op. cit., p. 46.   [5] John Dryden, op. cit., p. 55.

[6] John Dryden, 'Of Heroique Playes, An Essay' (*The Conquest of Granada*, 1672).

[7] Henri Prunière, *L'Opéra italien en France avant Lulli*, p. 168.

In a sense Bellori, whose *Lives of Painters* throws much light on the opinion of the period, exceeds Dryden in his views on nature. He asks that art shall excel over nature, that the total impression of a painting shall give a more perfect expression than the sum of the faulty parts imitated from objects as they are.[1] In literature, then, it follows that the heroic epic fulfils the requirements of such aesthetics more exactly than other types of poem. For in it the actions of mankind are imitated, but brought up to a 'nobler pitch'. The heroes are recognizable as human beings. But at the same time they are especially favoured, preserved for good or evil, set apart as examples to be imitated.

> Le Donne, i Cavalier, l'arme, gli amori,
> Le cortesie, l'audaci imprese io canto.

Such sentiments led librettists to take Ariosto and, of course, Tasso for the sources of many early plots. And it is significant that Monteverdi should have used a celebrated scene from the *Gerusalemme liberata* for his famous essay in the warlike genus, the *Combattimento di Tancredi e Clorinda*.

Even for such a short account it is possible to see that the aesthetic involved in the imitation of nature is based on a contradiction, since the nature that is to be imitated does not in effect exist. In it we can trace already the seeds of the romantic longing for the unattainable such as J. G. Robertson has seen in the immediate predecessors of Metastasio, such men as Vico and Gravina. But drama allied to music which, more than any other art, can 'move ye affections and excite passion',[2] does in some way resolve the problem. For if music, as Coleridge remarked, provides 'the fewest *analoga* in nature', and in fact Hadow says that 'so far as it relates to its subject, it could exist if there were no world of nature at all', it is 'an associated thing, and recalls the deep emotions of the past with an intellectual sense of proportion', for which it may be called 'the most entirely human of the fine arts'.[3] And therefore the fact that music is more exact, more definite in its powers than any other of the arts, whether due to its being an 'associated

---

[1] Giovanni Pietro Bellori, *Vite de' Pittori*, Pisa, 1628, vol. i, p. 8: 'Cosi l'Idea costituisce il perfetto della bellezza naturale, ed unisce il vero al verisimile delle cose sottoposte all' occhio, sempre aspirando all' ottimo, ed al maraviglioso, onde non solo emula, ma superiore farsi alla Natura.'

[2] The Hon. Roger North, *Musicall Gramarian*, reprinted from B.M. MS., London, 1925, p. 14.

[3] Sir Henry Hadow, *Studies in Modern Music*, First Series, p. 6.

[4] Samuel Taylor Coleridge, *On Poesy or Art* (*Biographia Literaria*, ed. Shawcross, vol. ii, p. 161).

thing' or not, gives it that quality which Dryden, for example, most desired in the arts, the power of elevating the mind and pleasing the senses of an audience. By dispensing with the need for imitation to attain such ends, the conflict between nature as it is and nature as he saw it should be, is obviated. The power of music, in fact, could do more to stir the emotions than the sight of a noble action on the stage. And it may be that this was a reason for the immense popularity of opera, the music of which could bring to life the stiff figures of heroic tragedy as spoken word could never do. In addition to the innate power of the music, the characters in an opera were bound to convey the superior quality of the epic from the very fact that, instead of speaking like the rest of mankind, they sang. Quite apart from the plot itself, any opera was bound to preserve the 'immeasurable gulf of shadows', which de Quincy places between the Greek audience and the great masked figures across the orchestra in the amphitheatre. And in this there may be a similarity between Greek drama and early opera. Doni, the learned librarian of the Vatican and a supporter of Monteverdi, makes it clear that supporters of monody look upon it as the most suitable means of making heard all the sentiments of the poetry 'without which the words are lost, and not in the fullness and sweetness of the harmony . . . the end of music not being to please but to stir up the affections.[1]'

However, the methods by which the early composers obtained a moving expression of human passion altered for succeeding generations as the aria encroached upon the recitative and arioso, the prevailing style in Monteverdi's operas and in the early works of Cavalli. And criticism such as Saint-Évremond passed later in his celebrated letters on opera begins to be heard. The librettist Sbarra considers that 'the ariette sung by Alexander and Aristotle are judged inappropriate to the dignity of characters so grand'. 'I know also', he continues, 'that it is improper to recite to music, since this method does not imitate natural speach and takes away the spirit of the dramatic piece which should be nothing else but an imitation of human actions. Indeed, this is not the only fault tolerated by the present age. But, received with applause, this class of poetry has no other end today but to please.

---

[1] Giovanni Battista Doni, *Compendio del Trattato de' generi e de' modi della musica*, Venice, 1635: 'Ma quelli sostengono la parte delle Monodie dicono che la perfectione della Musica consiste nel bello e gratioso cantare, e nel fare intendere tutti i sentimenti del poeta; senza che le parole si perdino; e non nella pienezza e suavita del Concento . . . non essendo il fine della Musica il Diletto, ma la commotione degl' Affetti.'

Therefore it suits itself to habits of the times. If the "stile recitativo" was not interspersed with suchlike amusements, it would bring more boredom than pleasure.'[1] Sbarra is referring to the change from the style of composition in which the melodic line takes on a more lyrical character at the demands of the text in certain situations; it may be called 'arioso'. And it grows out of the recitative as we can see from the short scene from Cavalli's opera *L'Egisto* (1643) in the music example No. 16. The clear-cut difference between recitative and aria which became the basis of subsequent Italian opera was considered by some critics to be too unnatural to accept. The distinction between the two styles is similar, although chronologically reversed, to that between an early opera by Verdi and *Otello* or *Falstaff*.

It seems curious that a librettist should betray the art that gives him a living in this way. But Sbarra's remarks are in fact contradictory. What he would appear to deplore is the increasing interruption in the 'stile recitativo' from the arietta. And the preface is an apologia in which he seems to be replying to critics who have complained of the number of these ariette on the grounds that they are contrary to nature, to which he agrees. But, in order to justify himself, although having originally agreed with his critics, he attempts to excuse this, as he considers it, lowering of standards to suit public taste on the grounds that the whole conception of opera is unnatural since it makes its characters behave unnaturally. And therefore, he seems to imply, he cannot be blamed for adding the ariette to an already absurd art. But he is only justified if he considers music to be an imitative art. Saint-Évremond's views on opera lead to the same fallacious conclusion.[2] He finds the necessity of singing everything from start to finish very difficult for the imagination to grasp because it is so unnatural. It is, he says, 'as if people in the opera had foolishly agreed to set to music all of life's activities, the humdrum along with the extraordinary'. But

---

[1] Francesco Sbarra; preface to *L'Alessandro vincitor di se stesso*. Drama musicale. Rappresentato in Venezia nel Theatro S. Gio e Paulo, 1651: 'Sò che l'ariette cantate da Alessandro e Aristotele si stimerano contro il decoro di personaggi si grandi, ma sò ancora ch'è improprio il recitarsi in Musica, non imitandosi in questa maniera il discorso naturale, e togliendosi l'anima al componimento Drammatico, che non deve esser altro, che un imitatione dell' attioni humane, e pur questo difetto non solo è tolerato del Secolo corrente: ma ricevuto con applauso, questa specie di Poesia hoggi non hà altro fine che dilettare, onde conviene accommodarsi all' uso dei Tempi; se lo stile recitativo non venisse intermezzato con simili scherzi, porterebbe più fastidio, che diletto.'

[2] *The Letters of Saint-Évremond*, ed. John Hayward, London, 1930, pp. 207 sqq.

both these authors mistake the function of music when they consider its main purpose to be that of imitating nature when its true purpose was to express passion and move the affections. It had no need of literal imitation; its powers lay in an ability to express various states of mind so that the audience could feel within themselves those emotions by which the characters in the plot were moved. In that sense only is music really imitative. The great mathematician Kircher considered it capable of expressing eight powerful affections—love, grief, joy, anger, pity, tears, fear, and admiration;[1] the Jesuit Schönsleder wrote a treatise in 1631 in which he tabulated the words suitable for special treatment.[2] Such treatment was common and in fact only by reason of it does much of the music of the seventeenth century become fully intelligible. Descartes, Mersenne, and Bannius testify in their writings to the importance of music used almost as a rhetorical device for explaining and elaborating words and states of mind.[3] The Royal Society in its early days discussed the minutiae of the degrees and qualities of sadness capable of differentiation through music. A member reading *An essay of making conjecture of dispositions by the voice* which attempts to show that 'sharps are effeminate; flats, a manly and melancholic sadness'.[4]

The aim to make music express a state of mind had important results in the actual composition, particularly of the arias. For it was considered that once the choice of mood was made, then the music had to express every degree or aspect of that state of mind, the mood itself being represented by an initial phrase in the score. It became more than 'la dolcezza e quasi l'anima della poesia', it became the key to the text, not so much the servant as the impresario.

---

[1] Athanasius Kircher, *Musurgia Universalis*, Rome, 1650, Bk. ix, p. 598: 'Octo potissimum affectus sunt, quos Musica exprimere potest. Primus est Amoris, Secundus Luctus seu Planctus. Tertius Laetitiae et Exsultationis. Quartus Furoris et Indignationis. Quintus, Commiserationis et Lacrymarum. Sextus, Timoris et Afflictionis. Septimus, Praesumptionis et Audaciae. Octavus, Admirationis. Ad quos omnia reliqua pathemata facile revocantur.'

[2] André Pirro, *L'Esthétique de J. S. Bach*, Paris, 1907, pp. 18–21.

[3] Much has been made of the theory of the affections. It is difficult to be certain of the exact meaning of the word. There seems to be some distinction between the passions and affections although it is hard to define. Kircher would appear to consider the Affection to be the state of mind which operates on the passion, for example Bk. ix, p. 600: 'Affectus Amoris est passio desiderii. Affectus doloris est passio animae.' But it seems unnecessary to go into the maze since the meaning of the term as far as the musician is concerned is perfectly clear from Monteverdi's prefaces and compositions.

[4] *Philosophical Transactions of the Royal Society*, No. 140, 1678.

Pallavicino, Galieno. Act III, 7. (1676)

CLORO

Hò ri-sol - to di non am-ar

rompo il la-ccio d'a - da-man - te

oc-chio bra - mo e lu-cen - te ces-si pur di

ba - le - nar ces-si pur di ba - le - nar

nu-me arcie-ro dà un ci-glio ne - ro saette avventami quan-to vuoi tu

sei fol - le sei fol - le se pen-si di vin-car mi più

sei fol - le sei fol - le se fol - le di vin-car mi più

An example from an opera *Galieno* by Pallavicino, a prolific Venetian composer, is a good illustration of this technique. The music of the aria derives from a four-note phrase of which the second is an auxiliary and the fourth alters its interval. But not only does this interval alternate between the third, fourth, fifth, sixth, and octave, but the stress alters as well, putting the auxiliary on to the beat. In the opening phrase for the voice the music is altered in that the quavers C to G of the theme previously announced on the continuo become crotchets. The importance of the bass is emphasized by its repetition after the first line of the libretto. The first part of the aria is completed at bar 6. The second part moves into A minor from C major and slightly changes its character. The jumps in thirds, no doubt to illustrate the destructive intentions of the text, continue. In fact, they lead to some bad part-writing in bars 11 to 14 to portray the flashing eyes at the word 'balenare'. At bar 18 the third section begins. The initial phrase, altered rhythmically, now plays a predominant part until the end, returning through the dominant back to C major. There is no development in this type of aria. It is analogous to the puzzles which can be found in Mersenne's writings.[1] Development in the manner of the classical composers is therefore foreign to the ideas of a seventeenth-century musician; there must be no statement followed by a working-out perhaps straying far from the original in order to make the return the more effective. On the contrary, the technique during the period of what is called the baroque, a period bounded roughly by Monteverdi and Bach, is analogous to that of the rhetoric, a parallel to which we drew attention in Chapter V. The initial figure is twisted and distorted into many differing attitudes, all variations of the original. Certain note formations are associated with certain states of mind, chromatic phrases, for example with grief, or a use of ornamentation to heighten the tension, methods which, depending upon the genius of the composer, have an impact of marvellous intensity. The clashes of harmony which are a feature of the music of the period can be explained as a rule either from the text or from the logic of two patterns interlocking, the notes of which may form the harshest discords. There

---

[1] Marin Mersenne, *Harmonie Universelle*, 'Des Chants', Proposition ix, p. 110: 'Determiner combien l'on peut faire de chants ou d'Airs differens avec six sons, ou six notes en prenant toujours les mesmes notes, et en gardant la mesme mesure.' He then gives a table of 720 variations of ut re mi fa sol la. Or again, p. 131, he gives 60 anagrams on the name of Jesus.

are many examples of such cases in the works of Bach,[1] which can be explained on these lines.

The effectiveness of these means depended ultimately, it was thought, on the connexion between the body and the soul, 'l'^me qui est liée au corps par des liens imperceptibles'.[2] And on this assumption is based the core of the ideas of imitation and nature as far as the idiom of music will allow. For even if the means of any art are limited, the effect is deep as well as far flung. And this is true particularly of opera, an art which combines the limited means of music, literature, and painting, and yet ranges, in its effect, over the whole gamut of human emotion.

It was by the restricted means of such figures as the chromatic ascent in the bass of the following example that the effect of profound grief was obtained.

The extreme clashes in harmony are justified only on the grounds of their expressive powers. Luzzo, the composer of this opera *Il Medoro*[3] (1658), could have explained his work on the lines indicated by Caccini in the preface to *Euridice* (1600). There he has 'not avoided the succession of two octaves or two fifths, thinking thereby, with their beauty and novelty, to cause a greater pleasure'.[4] Strict rules of counterpoint were beginning to be generally disregarded so long as the music gained in its power to express emotion. In Durante's *Arie devote* (1608) a

---

[1] Peter Platt, 'Melodic Patterns in Bach's Counterpoint', *M. and L.*, vol. xxix, January 1948.
[2] Claude Menestrier, *Des representations en musique anciennes et modernes*, Paris, 1682, p. 165.
[3] Act III. 22. Music example No. 18.
[4] Angelo Solerti, *Gli albori del melodrama*, vol. ii, p. 111 (tr. Strunk).

EXAMPLE 18. Luzzo–Aureli, *Il Medoro* (1658). Act III. 22

EXAMPLE 19. Sartorio–Aureli, *L'Orfeo* (1672). Act. II. 21

similar explanation is forthcoming, 'alle Arie si permette qualche licenza nel contrapunto per causa degli affetti'. And it is generally in the more poignant passages that the augmented and diminished intervals and chromatic intervals are to be found. Sartorio, the composer of *Orfeo*,[1] is particularly fond of such passages as this:

[1] Act II. 21. Music example No. 19.

The string accompaniment of these two examples itself is an indication that the composer wished to emphasize the importance of the passages as high-points in the emotional tension of the drama. The more usual method of expression is concentrated into the vocal line itself. Cavalli employs, for example, leaping fourths to express the wild cry of death in *Artemisia*[1] (1656) and contrasts the violence of it with the burden of grief expressed in a gentle sinking movement at 'che tante, tante pene':

Luzzo in *Medoro*[2] uses a similar technique from which any association with the older style of word-painting of the sixteenth century is broken. Here the music actually rises when a strict imitation of the text demands that it should fall. However, by rising and by the leap upwards of the tritone, the F sharp in the third bar becomes the first note of a sequential figure which gradually descends to give poignant expression to the anguish of the text.

A phrase from an aria in Boretti's *Claudio Cesare*[3] (1672) gives a more literal example of word painting in which the jump of the diminished intervals may be said to indicate the false appearance mentioned in the text.

[1] Act III. 4.   [2] Act III. 22.   [3] Act I. 4.

And an example from the early opera, *Le Nozze di Teti e di Peleo*[1] (1639) adheres even more closely.

Che scen-da à l'in-fer - no   al ciel sor-mon - to

The literal transcriptions often gave an opportunity for the virtuoso singer to show off his powers. For the librettists were careful to use language suitable for such passages, hence the circumscribed vocabulary found even in such masters of the art as Metastasio. Another extract from Sartorio's *Orfeo*[1] illustrates the word-painting on the word 'canto' and the emphasis given to the infernal kingdom ('regno infernal') by the sequentially rising figure which descends in a rapid scale passage.

Li - ra   il dolce can -   -   -   -

-    -   - to   accordi   e del Reg-no in-fer-nal _____

tra - mi   non   cu - ri.

From passages of this kind it is possible to discover more exactly what the seventeenth century understood by imitation, and to see the contradiction involved. There is, for example, a distinct difference between the literal transcription into notes of the words 'descent' and 'ascent', 'che scenda à l'inferno al ciel sormonto' in the example by Cavalli which corresponds more to the 'eye music', which Einstein describes as 'the most horrible testimony of naturalism',[2] a characteristic of the previous century, in his study *The Italian Madrigal*, something analogous to Mildmay Fane's collection of patterned poems *Otia Sacra* (1648), which is purely conventional, and that more platonic idea which treats 'man as a harp; the Powers and Faculties of the Soule, the strings; the Reason the harper', as Henry Hawkins describes the listener to the song of the Nightingale in *Partheneia Sacra*.[3] Here the imitation is expressive of the implications of language. The phrase which Sartorio sets for the word 'canto' is imitative, it is true, but only in a figurative sense. It would be possible to set the same phrase to the

---

[1] Act III. 4.   [2] Alfred Einstein, *The Italian Madrigal*, p. 234.
[3] *Partheneia Sacra*, by H. A., 1633, p. 140.

words 'regno infernal' which follow and to explain them on similar
lines. Likewise, this passage from Boretti's *Marcello in Siracusa*[1] (1670),
in which distance is rendered musically by wide leaps, is imitative
although, above other texts, it could be possible to interpret it as
equally an imitation unless, of course, it were possible to deduce from
other examples a scheme of note phrases that consistently appeared
above certain texts, as Pirro and Schweitzer contend is the case with
J. S. Bach. But there is no strict rule to be found in the works of the
Venetian school. It can only be stated that certain awkward phrases
are brought about by textual imitation on the one hand, or through a
need to capture the mood, as a means of expression, on the other.

One final example comes from *Medea in Atene*[2] (1673) by Zannettini.
The word 'courage' is given a little flourish and the glance of the eyes,
'raggio de gl' occhi', finds expression by means of a *gruppo* or trill.

But, unless it were possible to discover that these words and the
like were always set in a particular formula, as it were, there is no

[1] Act I. 5.   [2] Act I. 2.

justification in ascribing an exact meaning to any one phrase in the manner of a conventional sign.

The imitation of nature, then, in the music of the time is concerned with expression: ultimately, as in the Pastoral Symphony it is 'mehr Ausdruck der Empfindung als Malerey'. The connexion between text and music is in fact a parallelism which 'can also be present when externally the opposite seems to be presented—that, for example, a tender thought can be expressed by a quick and violent theme because the following violence will develop from it more organically. . . '.[1] It is often held that between Monteverdi and Gluck there was little attempt made by composers to use music as a means of expression because the vocal line became over-florid or the harmonic idiom was insufficiently understood. Whereas, in fact, the intention behind the music of the seventeenth-century opera-house was very much the expression of mood.

Occasionally there are, it is true, passages in which the orchestra itself is called upon to play a descriptive part. The celebrated incantation scene from Cavalli's *Giasone* and the 'concilio infernale' in his *Le Nozze di Teti e di Peleo* are accessible in print.[2] Grossi uses the strings in a more exactly imitative sense in *Nicomede in Bitenia*[3] (1677), where

---

[1] Arnold Schoenberg, *Style and Idea*, London, 1951, p. 3.

[2] Robert Eitner, *Gesellschaft für Musikforschung*, vol. xii for the score of *Giasone*. *O.H.M.*, vol. iii, p. 169 gives the scene. *O.H.M.*, vol. iii, p. 131 and Robert Haas, *Die Musik des Barocks*, p. 134, print the 'concilio infernale'.

[3] Act I. 24.

the blows of the hammer find a counterpart in the aria sung by the sculptor as he chips at the stone.

Although the choice of instruments specifically for reasons of tone-colour is rare, but not unknown, the same effect which in the mid-eighteenth century was sought through painting nature by means of instrumental colour was gained in the seventeenth century through the use of these expressive figures allied to the texts. The accompanied arioso which composers used to intensify the song in moments of extreme poignancy 'dont l'Harmonie est confuse, chargée de Modulations et Dissonance', as Rousseau understands 'une Musique Baroque',[1] is a nursery for the triumphant instrumental music which ultimately superseded the hegemony of the human voice. The adjective rhetorical which has already been used to describe the technique, which, so to speak, plays about with a phrase without developing it, could be used to describe all music of the *seconda pratica* from *c.* 1600, marking a change in the demands made upon music. Count Giovanni Bardi, around whom were grouped the members of the famous Florentine Camerata at the turn of the century, hailed Cipriano da Rore as one of the first composers to understand the expressive style.[2] Monteverdi himself gives Rore the credit of first writing music considering 'harmony not commanding, but commanded'.[2] Similarly, rhetoric is itself the art of speaking effectively. Consequently the bonds between music of the seventeenth century and that of the subsequent age are very strong. Imitation used in a musical sense is, in fact, after the late sixteenth century, nothing but expression. The identification of the two terms is of great significance in the new alliance between music and words.

Sismondi considered that 'the rise of opera may, perhaps, be considered as the only literary event of the seventeenth century of which Italy can justly boast'.[3] It stimulated poets in a deeper sense than the mere need to fulfil a popular desire. There was very little civil liberty in any Italian State and the expression of opinion or of controversial ideas had in some way to find an outlet. The epic whether drawn from mythology or ancient history provided an easy subterfuge; even Tasso's *Aminta* clothed in pastoral guise members of the court of

[1] Jean Jacques Rousseau, *Dictionnaire de Musique*, see under 'Baroque'.

[2] Foreword to the 1607 edition of the fifth book of Madrigals, tr. Strunk, op. cit., p. 409.

[3] Jean Sismonde De Sismondi, *Historical View of the Literature of the South of Europe*, tr. Roscoe, London, 1823, vol. ii, p. 209.

Mantua. The mind was quick to catch an allusion; symbols and images were readily understood and appreciated, a whole world lay readily at hand.

In general, the reflections on contemporary life were hidden under the deeds of some hero of far-off days, a Scipio or a Titus; these figures were made to behave according to contemporary standards and to be conscious of their importance as examples to a subsequent age; for instance, Aeneas, conscious of his future countrymen and fearful lest they should see in his flight from Troy a certain weakening in civic pride, is aware of this responsibility when he appeals to future genera-tions of Italians:

> O' seculi venturi
> Da voi sempre si giuri,
> Ch'io non manco al dover di Cittadino,
> Ma presto ossequio al commandar divino.

Busenello, the author of this *Didone* (1641), the first and most impor-tant dramatist of the Venetian stage, constantly puts such histrionic rantings into the mouths of his heroes. Anachronisms, too, are frequent. Socrates walks proudly up the steps of the royal palace at Athens and high-born Roman ladies look forward to the resolution of amorous complications beneath the shadow of the nun's veil. The Abbé d'Aubignac was quick to notice that[1] 'if there be any Act or Scene that has not that conformity of manners to the Spectators, you will sud-denly see the applause cease'. Later, Horace Walpole was to comment on this habit in the writings of his friend Mason who had imitated the greatest Italian librettist. 'Sappho', he says, 'must not utter the word *requiem*: in short, Metastasio may use such an anachronism, but Musaeus must not, shall not.'[2] However, although theorists con-sidered verisimilitude to be of importance, and indeed, as far as the production was concerned, some care was taken to present an opera in its historical setting, the fundamental aim was 'not to present things as they have been but as they ought to be'.[3] By such means alone was a stage spectacle really effective. It was felt that stories from a more or less remote past provided an association 'from whence th' Inlightened spirit sees That shady City of Palme trees' which time seemed to have purged of evil. And, although the figures behaved in a curiously

---

[1] M. Hedelin Abbot (*sic*) of Aubignac, *The Whole Art of the Stage*, tr. London, 1684, p. 72.
[2] To Rev. William Mason, 24 January 1778.   [3] Abbé Hedelin, op. cit., p. 65.

modern way, it was somehow felt that they were in a sense divested, by reason of their antiquity alone, of any contact with original sin. The pastoral subjects which lingered over into the second half of the seventeenth century, although far less popular than the heroic, were the object of a warning by Doni. The shepherds in these plots are not, he says, to be confused with 'the squalid vulgar lot who guard the animals today':[1] they must resemble those of the old days when the occupation was the preserve even of the highest-born. This tradition is carried into the stories from history, medieval and classical, by the simple means of presenting the characters, whoever they are, as types. The villain deserves to draw out the full magnanimity of the hero, and is himself in the denouement converted to righteousness by the clemency of his intended victim. Thus the monsters and heroes, the Caligulas and Scipios of history, are sucked into the honeycomb of universal benignity. In one sense the music aids this hallucination for it heightens the distance between what is and what should be, or more accurately what has been, particularly if we remember that according to many contemporary authorities on the earliest history of mankind such as Vico, song had been the first means of human expression.[2] In the other sense, of course, the music kept the conventions within the bounds of possibility through its convincing powers of expression. The stiff characters became true to life because the music created a response within the faculties of the audience. Although the plot seemed to be dealing with heroes, 'brought up to a nobler' pitch, in fact the emotions and situations were those within the experience of the audience themselves.

The setting for an opera was able to combine this realism with an element of phantasy, making the representation the more effective. An attention to details, an attempt to imitate the habits and customs of those represented was the inheritance from the previous century when the designers were advised to imitate the scenery natural to the scene and to adapt the clothes according to local customs.[3] But the

---

[1] Giovanni Battista Doni, De' Trattati di Musica, ed. Gori (1763), vol. ii, Trattato della Musica Scenica, p. 16: 'non debbiano immaginarci, che i pastori che s'introducono, siano di questi sordidi, e volgari, che oggi guardano il bestiame; ma quelli del secolo antico, nel quale i più nobili esercitavano quest' arte.'   [2] Giovanni Battista Vico, Scienza Nuova, Bk. I, sec. ii, lix.

[3] Angelo Ingegnieri, Della Poesia rappresentativa, Ferrara, 1598, pp. 62 sqq.: 'La Scena deve assimigliarsi il più che sia possibile al luoco, dove si finge, che sia avvenuto il case, di cui è composta la favola . . . sarà per tanto da vedere in qual paese si finga la favola, che si rappresenta ; a seconda l'usanza di quella natione si dovranno vestire i recitanti.'

new design for the theatre itself in which the play was acted within the framework of the proscenium arch and separated from the audience by the orchestral pit, made certain that the action was different from that of ordinary life. It was presented as a picture in a frame with the knowledge that 'les yeux sont tout-puissants sur l'âme', as Madame de Staël was to make Corinne inform Lord Nelvil.

In practice, dress seems to have been stylized with the obvious uses of conventional attributes where such details have been associated in popular imagination with the character or country concerned. It is difficult to assess the degree of imitation in the sets themselves since few have survived. Torelli alters little but the background in his designs for *La Finta Pazza* and *Il Bellerofonte* in the Paris and Venice productions. In the one he shows the Pont Neuf and in the other the Piazetta. But, apart from the familiar background in each, there is no other attempt at realism. As far as imitation is concerned he seems to have shown very little interest. Although one of the foremost designers, he is of an older generation than the artists who were concerned with the sets for the historical plots: plots which portray the real attitude of the seventeenth-century dramatists and musicians to the problem of verisimilitude and nature. The description of the opening scene of *Doriclea*[1] (1645) is a more typical example of the contemporary attitude. For in it the description reads as a page from a gazetteer. It was certainly intended to be read with care since the course of the river could not be shown on the stage. And the details included, such as the whereabouts of its source and mouth, could have no real bearing on the actual plot. Yet such descriptions form part of every libretto and were obviously a delight to the audience. They provided an atmosphere of reality to the performance and at the same time insured that it remained somehow apart from it. Perspective itself, upon which the art of stage design depended, had a similar effect on the audience for it created a phantasy along which the imagination could wander. In a sense it fulfilled a similar office to the aria which allowed the imagination full play to dwell on the situation presented by the action in recitative. The opera, in fact, truly reflects the spirit of *seicento* Italy, by providing a satisfactory medium for a duality which above all seeks new methods of expression, new excitements, yet is afraid to acknowledge that the present can provide them. The spirit

[1] See p. 67.

of humanism had sufficient power still to make men think of the classical age as the apogee of human endeavour. But much of the allegiance was lip-service only. For the heroes were no longer demi-gods who could wander freely over the earth, they were humans raised up by art. The modern poetic spirit endeavoured, in fact, to 'hold the affections of others in excitement through novelty, deducing from things true or seemingly true, things never thought or known of before'.[1] Venetian music played its full part in the development and fulfilment of these canons of taste. For Venice was described as a city 'où les Theatres sont si propres, les decorations si belles, et si diversifiées, les machines si justes, les voix si agreables, La musique si sçavante, et si bien ajustée aux passions, et aux affections de l'Ame',[2] which fulfilled the requirements of the intellect and the senses to contemporary satisfaction.

[1] Francesco Quadrio, *Della storia e della ragione d'ogni poesia*, Bologna, 1739, vol. i, p. 348: 'Anzi questo è il carattere veramente dello spirito poetico procurar sempre con la novità di tener in agitazione gli altrui affetti; deducendo da cose vere, o verisimili, cose o non pensate o non sapute giammai; ed esser vario, multiplice, versipelle, in variare per maraviglia continua gli animi, vibrarli, e sospenderli.'

[2] Claude Menestrier, *Des representations en musique anciennes et modernes*, Paris, 1681, p. 165.

Archivio di Stato, Venice. Busta no. 914 (Teatri varii)

Extracts from the notebooks of the Secretaries to the Town Councils of Crema and Bergamo, both at the time under Venetian rule

The comparative value of currencies in the seventeenth century is difficult to assess. Venetian money and its relative value amongst the Italian states is explained in N. Papadopoli's scholarly book *Sul valore della moneta veneziana.* In the lira veneta there are 20 soldi each worth 240 denari. The Ducat is worth 6 lire 4 soldi. And the filippo in the Bergamo accounts equals the lira in value. We know from a marginal note in a document from the Public Record Office that in 1670 a ducat was worth 3*s.* 10*d.,*[1] which would make the lira worth about 7½*d.* However, knowledge of this nature is not really useful. A comparison of wages and prices, outside the scope of this book, is the only valuable means of understanding monetary relations.

Extract from the minutes of the Town Council of Crema, 17 September 1681.

Whereas, according to the decision of the General Council of the city on 15 September of this year, two small houses have been bought which used to belong to the heirs of the late Signor Antonio Maria Monza—situated near the Piazze Maggiori and touching on the south side of the new building—used for public archives and for other purposes, without which houses it would have been impossible to achieve [our aim], that the agreement for their purchase has been made public through the notary, Sig. Fulvio BREMASCO on the 16th of the same month, and whereas, following valid reasons given by the Illmo et Ecc^{mo} Sig. Antonio Canale, at present Podestà and Capitanio of the same city, work has been done to establish there a theatre for the use of the actors and for the honour of the city. Thirty-eight boxes have been built in it, namely, 19 in the first row and as many in the second, the two central ones are intended, that in the first row for the Ill^{mi} et Ecc^{mi} Rettori during their time of office (local administrators), that in the second for the Ill^{mi} Proveditori equally whilst in office and the other boxes are to be distributed by lot, drawn in the presence of his Excellency (Podestà), the Ill^{mi} Proveditori and of many gentlemen from those who attempted to have them, by paying ten filippi each, for those of the first row, and eight for those of the second row, on the condition that they remain for ever as their own property and the property of their heirs and successors and that they are allowed to make use of them whenever and however they please, and to dispose of them even to others provided the buyer belongs to the council or is a Venetian Nobleman. In order that any confusion should be always avoided and that everyone should know exactly what place has been allotted to him, the same Ill^{mi} Proveditori have ordered the present book to be prepared in which the names are put down of

---

[1] Transcript from *State Papers Foreign, Venice,* 99/47, fol. 147.

those to whom the boxes have been allotted with their numbers and to this book complete trust must always be given,

Curtio CLAVELLO Proveditori
Cosmo BENVENUTI   „
Allessandro OBIZI   „

Archivio di Stato. Busta no. 914. Minutes and accounts of the Town Council of Crema.

D. Vitruvio Alberi must give a sum equal to that received by him from the individuals to whom the boxes of the new theatre have been assigned

For those in the 1st row	L.1,564: –
„ „ „ „ 2nd „	L.1,173: –
Interest on filippi No. 63	L. 6: 6
	L.2,743: 6

Sig: Gio. Battista Comincini must give a sum equal to that received by him from the below-mentioned according to the receipt (filed) from

Nob Sig Bartolomeo Valente for Box No. 21 . . .	L. 73: –12
Nob Sign Annibale & brothers Vim^ti No. 6	L. 92: –
Nob Sig Hettone Vim^ti for the box belonging to late	
Nob Sig Benedetto S(?) Gio: Tosetti (?) e (Sig Gaspero?) No. 28	L. 73: –12

Sig Alberi must receive a sum equal to that paid, as below, to Illmo et Ecc^mo Sig Antonio Caual, Podestà et Capitanio as from his receipt in the file L.2,054: 7

Agostino Bonetto, Stonemason for the price of marble stairs as from receipt in the file . . . . L. 420: –

Master Joachino Vella for bricks as from receipt in the file . . L.   72: –

Master Bernado Antonetto for work done on the stairs as from receipt in the file . . . . L. 134: –

Ser Carlo Chiesa, Bailiff (massarolo?) for help as from receipt in the file . . . . L.   26: –

Men who have cleared the plaster by order of the Ill^mi Sig^i Provedi-tori . . . . L.   4: –

Master Domenico Morello for background (sfondro) . . . L.   27: 18

	L.2,738: 5
Sundries (resta)	L. 5: 1
	L.2,743: 6

The above mentioned Sig Comincini must receive in lire a hundred
and sixteen and four as the cost of eighty-three ells[1] of planks of
'pigera' bought from Nob Sign Ettore Vin^{ti} at L.1. 8 an ell . L. 116: 4
and hundred and twenty three lire handed to the Ecc^{mo} Podestà
Canal to pay for struts and for the workers as from the list in the
file . . . . L. 123:

L. 239: 4

Money received from Sig^i to whom the boxes of the new theatre
have gone by lot and handed to the Illmo et Ecc^{mo} Antonio Canale
Podestà et Capitanio of Crema by order of the Illmo Sigi Proveditori
by hand of D. Vitruvio Alberi, Bedel of the city, for the building of
the theatre and for the boxes for the same, two thousand and fifty
four lire, seven soldi L.2,054: 7

Signed: ANTONIO CANAL. PODESTÀ CAPITANIO

His Illustrious Excellency has spent in the building of the theatre and boxes two
thousand and sixty four lire and one soldo as from seven bills handed by his Excellency to the Ill^{mi} Sig^i Proveditori with the bill receipted by the workers and the
people who have sold the materials namely

Master Bernardo, Mason L.153: 12
    Vincenzo Premoli for timber L.561: 12
    Carlo Pelolio, Smith L.129: 8
    Marc' Antonio Grosso, Ironmongery L.175: 15
    Master Cristoforo Barile, Mason L.189: 10
    Carlo Antonio Palenera, Carpenter, for work done and timber L.715: 0
    Another of the same L.139: 4

L.2,064: 1

In addition there is all the plaster squared for facings and for the floor stones (salizo),
sand for the making of the facings which, through the generosity of the above-named
Excellency, have been given free for the same building of the above-mentioned
theatre.

8th January 1683.

In the big hall of the Town Hall (Palazzo) and in the presence of Illmo et Ecc^{mo} Sig
Antonio Ottobon Podestà et Capitaniò, after the ringing of the bell, the General
Council met and was found by the public Bedel to be of the number of 92 councillors.
The document below written was read as it had been proposed by the Illmo Sig^{ri}
Proveditori and already discussed in the smaller council, according to the orders on
the 5th of this month, and which, having been opposed by the Ecc^{mo} Sig Dott
Giovanni Francesco Albergone 'Publico Contradittor' and by the Ecc^{mo} Sig Dott
Juilio Cesare Braguti, was not voted upon but in its stead—consideration being paid
to the different arguments arising amongst the councillors—the new document was

[1] One ell = 46 inches.

proposed by His Illustrious Excellency which is transcribed below which, having been approved by vote, was accepted with sixty-five votes in favour and twenty-three against.

After several decrees of this council 7th January and 29th June 1678 a building was approved at the south of the big archway of the Piazze Maggiori so that by balancing the Palazzo it would add beauty to the building; it should be used for archives and repository of documents, minutes, acts of notaries, books, measures and accounts of the surveyors of the public lands which things are being dispersed with prejudice to private and public good, and also as the seat of the Academy, Magistracies, pawn chamber and for other purposes. After the building was started and well on the way, and since it was realised that in order to make it more perfect and to make it possible that it should include a theatre for actors without excluding the Academy, it was necessary to buy the two small houses belonging to the heirs of Sig Antonio Maria Monza touching it. And it was also, in a document of 15th September 1681, decided to buy it and purchase was carried out the following day.

Following the effective pressure of the Illmo and Ecc^mo Sig Antonio Canale, then Podestà and Capitanio of the City, work was started on the building of the Theatre. Two rows of boxes (thirty-eight in all) were also built, including one in each row situated in the middle opposite the stage; the one in the first row being reserved for the Ill^mi and Ecc^mi Publici Representanti during their term of office, and the one in the second row being reserved to the Ill^mi Signori Proveditori, equally during their term of office; the other thirty-six would be reserved to several Gentiluomini who have entered a competition for them, by paying 10 filippi each for those of the first row and eight filippi for those of the second row, according to the decree of Our Precessori, 17th September 1681; and distributed through an extraction by lot, in order to avoid disorders and confusion between the competitors, the extraction being done in front of the Illmo and Ecc^mo Signor Podestà and Capitanio with the assistance of our Precessori on the 24th of the same month. A few which have been given up were allotted to other Gentiluomini by us the Proveditori. But in order that things should be more stable, and that it should be possible to improve the Theatre and the Archive, this Council will decide that the distribution of the above-mentioned boxes and the substitutions done by us are approved and confirmed with all the conditions set out by the mentioned decree of 17th September, which is going to be read together with this present statement, for everybody's more complete enlightenment. The book of these distributions has to be put in order, and kept in the Chancellery of the City, for the perpetual establishment of this order.

It will be the task of the Signori Proveditori in office to discuss and take advice with other Citizens who understand and are expert in these things, whether other boxes can be added in that theatre; and if so, they will have full power to have them built, to distribute them to the subjects (members) of this Council, and, failing these, to other Citizens of some standing, for the price which they think should be paid into the hands of the Bedel of this City, at the act of the assignation.

If boxes are going to be built at the ground level of the theatre, below those already built, the aforesaid Signori Proveditori should not allow that benches should be put in the pit, which could prevent the seeing of the stage, but simple chairs must be put, or stools, or benches not higher than 15 'oncias'[1] and these seats should always be at the disposal of the City.

All the money earned in this way, should be paid at the act of the distribution of these new boxes, into the hands of a Bedel, and reserved absolutely for improvements in the Theatre and Archive in the way to be decided by the Signori Proveditori in office, under the penalty that whosoever acts differently will have to pay out of his own pocket, because it must be arranged that in all ways possible this labour ('fatica'), of such an urgency, should be brought to perfection, which has been carried so far with so much dignity ('decoro') for the fatherland and to everybody's satisfaction.

(The document mentioned above, proposed by His Illustrious Excellency and approved, as stated above, follows here.)

The Illmo and Ecc^{mo} Sig^r Antonio Ottobon Podestà and Capitanio etc. asks whether the Theatre must be built or not, since the erection of the theatre in the place of the Academy (without however excluding the Academy itself) must depend on the will of this council.

15th January 1683.

In the Great Hall of the Palazzo, the General Council met in the presence of the Illmo and Ecc^{mo} Sig^r Antonio Ottobone Podestà and Capitanio; their number, as counted by the Public Bedel, was found to be 82 councillors.

The following document, submitted by the Ill^{mi} Sig^{ri} Proveditori, was read; the public contradictor, the Ecc^{mo} Sig^r Dr. Clavello Calvelli, according to his duty, contradicted it; then it was voted upon, and approved with sixty-two votes against twenty.

Whereas, through a decision of this Council 8th January of this year, the erection has been approved of the new Theatre, without however excluding the Academy; and whereas 38 boxes have already been built in it, and distributed in the way, form, and with the conditions set out in the decree of our Precessori 17th September 1681; and whereas it was suggested that there is room in the Theatre for other boxes, which—if built and distributed—would yield money enough, not only for the completion of the Theatre itself, but also for the progress on the Archive, already decided upon, and so necessary.

It will be decided that:—

It will be the task of us the Proveditori and our successors in office, to discuss and take advice with other understanding and expert Citizens, as to whether other boxes can be added comfortably, and in such a case, whether they should be built and distributed to subjects (members) of this Council and other Citizens of some standing, for the price of eight or ten filippi, as will be considered better; and this money should be paid into the hands of the Treasurer of the City at the moment of the assignation; and this money must be absolutely reserved and expended exclusively for the completion of the Theatre and Archive, in the way in which the Proveditori will think best, under the penalty that whosoever orders differently should pay of his own.

---

[1] The *oncia* is $\frac{1}{2}$ of a *piede*.

If new boxes are to be built on the floor level of the Theatre and under those which are already there, it will be the task of the above mentioned Proveditori in office not to allow that benches should be placed in the pit such as would impede the sight of the stage; there should be only simple chairs and stools, and benches not higher than fifteen 'oncias'; and these seats must remain for ever at the disposal of the City.

16th January 1682.

The Ill^mi Sig^ri Francesco Monte, Aloysio Zurla and Ferdinando Vimercati Proveditori of this City, having heard the request made by the Noble Signor Ettore Vimercati, in his and other Noble Citizens' names, asking that permission should be given to him and the others by Sue Signorie Illustrissime for an opera to be produced several times in the new theatre of this City, permission has been granted to the mentioned Signor Ettore for that opera to be produced in that theatre during the whole of the present Carnival. Decided upon and published in the Hall of the Chancellery of the City, in the presence of Fran(cesco) Tesino and Fran(cesco) Tacca.

9th April 1682.

The Ill^mi Sig^ri Francesco Monte, Aloysio Zurla and Ferdinando Vimercati Proveditori of this City, having heard the request made by the Noble Dr. Ettore Vimercati in his and other Citizens' names, asking for a permit to be granted to him and the others by Sue Signorie Illustrissime for an opera to be produced several times in the new theatre of this City, permission is hereby granted to the above mentioned Sig^r Ettore in his name, as above stated, to have that opera produced in this theatre during the whole of the present month.

In the presence of Vitruvio Alteri and Giovanni Battista Marchi.

1st May 1683.

Whereas the Illustrissimi Nobili Provveditori have been asked by the Nobile Signor Ettore Vimercate, in the name of some Citizens of initiative, who would like to produce in the Theatre of this City an opera bearing the title of La Pallia Politica de Rodrigo Re di Cicilia,[1] therefore the Ill^mi Nobili Giovanni Battista Terni and Ercole Monteslino, also in the name of the Illmo Dr. Niccolò Maria Benzone Provveditori have graciously granted permission to the above mentioned Dr. Ettore to have this opera produced. In the presence of the Noble Giovanni Battista Marchi and Vitruvio Alteri.

16th September 1684.

The Ill^mi N^li Antonio Maria Clavelli, Giovanni Battista Monteslini, and Count Carlo Premili, Provveditori of this City, following the respectful requests submitted orally to them by the Noble Ambroggio Broglia and Compagni Comici, asking for a permit to produce in the main theatre of this City several operas and comedies during the next two months, have granted to the same the mentioned permission. Witnesses the Noble Francesco Tinare and Carlo Malosio.

26th January 1686.

The Ill^mi N^li Curtio Benvenuti and Aloysio Zurla, also in the name of Sig^r

---

[1] There is no trace of this opera in Sonneck or Allacci.

Ludovico Vincenzo San^{no} Proveditori of this City, following the respectful requests submitted by Sig^r Antonio Scappi, asking for a permission to produce in the theatre of this City an opera in music for the whole of the present Carnival, have granted and grant by the present act the permission requested, reserving however for themselves the first three rows of stools in front, and also the right of having another opera produced during that period for some appointed days, according to a permission already granted to other people; they also demand that Signor Scappi should deliver every evening in which the opera is produced one 'bulletin' for each of the Proveditori, i.e. one entrance ticket for them to dispose of in the way they like. In the presence of the Nobili Signori Alessandro Zurla and Giacomo Achille Zurla.

17th July 1686.

The Ill^{mi} Sig^{ri} Curtio Benvenuto and Camillo Scotti, two of the Ill^{mi} Signori Proveditori, in acceptance of the respectful requests submitted by Sig^r Filippo Giuliani, who proposes to give some variety entertainment in the theatre of this City, have granted and grant a permission for them to be able to use the theatre for the whole of this month of July for the above specified aim.

Witnesses Giovanni Battista Marchi and Ser Carlo Chiesa.

24th May 1687.

Whereas it had been decided, with several decrees of the General Council of this City, 8 and 15 January 1683, that the Proveditori in charge should discuss with, and take advice from, other expert citizens about the possibility of adding other boxes in the Theatre, and that they should have full power to have them built and distributed to members of the mentioned Council, or failing these to other prominent citizens, at a price considered right, i.e. eight or ten filippi, to be paid at the time of assignation, and whereas we, Niccolò Maria Benzone, Agostino Monte, and Ferdinando Zurla, the present Proveditori, have discussed this question with many people who agreed that it is possible to build sixteen boxes on the (ground) floor to be added to the two near the stage for the use of the Musicians and actors, and five more above those already built opposite the stage, following the request of prominent members, we decree that those boxes, to the number of twenty-one, are to be built; and those who give their names to one of the Cancellieri for the purpose of obtaining them will have to pay eleven ducats for each box, into the hands of Vittorino Albero, Bedel, within eight days after the drawing of the lot; for the distribution of the boxes should be done by lots (with the exception of two boxes which will be assigned by the Illmo and Ecc^{mo} Sig. Co: Gelio Piovene Podestà and Capitanio, and the other by the Ecc^{mo} Sig. Danide Balbi Camerlengo), and the lots shall be drawn in the presence of the Illmo and Ecc^{mo} Sig. Podestà and Capitanio, and of anybody who cares to be present, so that there should be no complaint.

Niccolò Maria Benzone, Proveditore.
Agostino Monte, Proveditore

Archivio di Stato, Venice. Busta no. 914. (*Teatro di Bergamo*)

Extract from the ledger of the Town Council accounts, 13 *October* 1687

Sig^re Gaspero Torelli of Venice must have the current value in ducats (ducati corenti) at six lire four soldi.[1] L. one thousand one hundred and fifty for the contract to make the stage, machines, painting of the scenes and besides all that appears in the written agreement of the Illmo and Ecc^mo Sig Podestà and Cap°.   F.7130:

In addition F.700 as the agreement made for having painted all the ceiling, proscenium and exterior of the theatre   F. 700:
    [then follows a list of unspecified items paid to his account]
Sig Gasparo Torelli must have for such items from this account 14   F.7882:

13th Oct. 1687. For having had made the stools for the theatre   F. 248:
And for the floor of the theatre   F. 167: 8.
                                                                        ───────
                                                                        F.8297: 8.

                          Agostino Monte   P^re
                          Hicoto   Scritt^r. Prod^a

---

[1] This is a practical reference to a decree of the Venetian Senate of 1687 for currency stabilization in which the ducat was fixed at 6 lire 4 soldi. Cf. Papadopoli, op. cit., p. 24.

Nicola Sabbattini, 'Pratica di Fabricar Scene, e Machine ne' Teatri', Ravenna, 1638

The book is divided into two parts: the first shows the methods of construction of the theatre and sets, whereas the second deals with the machines and stage effects.

Index to chapter headings

Cap. 54. Come si possa rappresentare un Paradiso.

Cap. 55. Modo di far nascere l'Aurora.

Cap. 56. Come si possa far comparire, ò sparire un'Ombre [*sic*], ò Fantasima in diversi luoghi sopra il piano del Palco con prestezza.

Cap. 57. Della facilità della Pratica.

Andromeda

Description of scenes, &c., taken from the edition of 6 May 1637, two months after the first performance

Sparita la Tenda si vide la Scena tutta mare; con una lontananza così artifituosa d'acque, e di scogli, che la naturalezza, di quella (ancor che finta) movea dubbio à Riguardanti, se veramente soffero in un Teatro, ò in una spiaggia di mare effetiva. Era la Scena tutta oscura, se non quanto le davano luce alcune stelle; le qualiuna dopo l'altra à poco à poco sparendo, dettero luogo all' Aurora, che venne à fare il Prologo. Ella tutta di tela d'argento vestita, con una stella lucidissima in fronte, comparve dentro una bellissima nube, quale hora dilatandosi, hora stringendosi (con bella meraviglia) fece il suo passaggio in arco per lo Ciel della Scena. In questror mentre si vede la Scena luminosa à par del giorno. Dalla Signora Madalena Manelli Romana fù divinamente cantato il Prologo: dopo del quale s'udi de più forbiti Sonatori una soavissima Sinfonia; à questi assistendo l'Autore dell' Opera con la sua miracolosa Tiorba. Uscì depoi Giunone sovra un carro d'oro tirato da suoi Pauoni, tutta vestita di tocca d'oro fiammante, con una superba varietà, di gemme in testa, e nella corona. Con meravigliosa diletto, de spettatori volgeva à destra, ed'à sinistra, come più le piaceva, il carro. Le comparve à fronte Mercurio. Era, e non era questo Personaggio in machina; Era, perche l'impossibilità non l'ammetiva volante; e non era, poiche niun altra machina si vedea, che quella del corpo volante. Comparve guernito de suoi soliti arnesi, con un manto azurro, che le gioa sciolazzando alle spalle. Fù eccelentemente rappresentate Giunone dal Signor Francesco Angeletti da Assisi; ed esquisitamente Mercurio dal Signor Don Annibale Graselli da Città di Castello. In un istante si vide la Scena, di maritima, Boschereccia; così del naturale ch'al vivo al vivo ti portava all' occhio quell' effettiva cima nevosa, quel vero pian fiorito, quella reale intrecciatura del Bosco e quel non finto scioglimento d'acque. Comparve Andromeda con il seguito, di dodeci Damigelle, in habito Ninfale. L'habito d'Andromeda era di color, di foco, d'inestimabile valuta. Quello delle Ninfe era bianco, incarrato, e Oro. Rappresentò mirabilmente Andromeda chi fece il Prologo. Tornò in un momento la Scena, di Boschereccia, Maritima. Comparve Nettuno, e gli uscì Mercurio nella sua mirabil machina all' incontro. Era Nettuno sovra una gran Conca d'argento, tirata da quattro cavalli marini. Lo copriva un manto di color cilestre: una gran barba gli scendeva al petto, e una lunga capillatura inghirlandata d'alga le pendeva alle spalle. La corona era fatta à Piramidette, tempestata di perle. Fece questa parte egregiamente il Signor Francesco Manelli da Tivoli; autore della Musica, dell' Opera. Uscì dal seno del mare, dalla cintola insuso, Protheo, vestito à squamme d'argento; con una gran capillatura, e barba di color ceruleo. Servi di questo Personaggio gentilissimamente il Signor Gio: Battista Bisucci Bolognese. Qui per fine dell' Atto si cantò prima di dentro un Madrigale à più voci, concertato con Istrumenti diversi; e poi tre bellissimi Giovinetti, in habito d'Amore, uscirono à fare, per Intermezzo, una gratiosissima danza. Il velocissimo moto, di questi fanciulli tallora fece dubbiose le Genti, s'havessero eglino l'ali à gli homeri, ò pure à piedi. A tempo, d'una melliflua melodia, di stromenti, comparvero Astrea nel Cielo, e Venere nel mare. Una entro una nube d'argento; l'altra nella sua conca, tirata da Cigni. Era vestita Astrea del color del Cielo, con una spada à fiamme nella destra. Venere del color del mare, con un manto d'oro incarnato alle spalle. Fù gratiosamente rappresentata Astrea del Signor Girolamo Medici Romano, e Venere soavissimamente dal Signor Anselmo Marconi Romano. Si mutò la Scena in Boschereccia, e uscì Andromeda con la sua schiera. Sei delle sue Dame, qui per allegrezza dell' ucciso Cinghiale, fecero un leggiadro, e maraviglioso Balletto; con si varie, e mirabili intrecciature, che veramente gli si poteva dar nome, d'un laberinto saltante. Ne fù l'Inventore il Signor Gio: Battista Balbi Venetiano, Ballarino celebre. Uscì repente di sottoterra Astarco Mago, com'Ombra. Era questo Personaggio tutto vestito à bruno d'oro, veste lunga, con capillatura, e barba lunga, e come neve bianca. Scettro di Negromante, reggeva la destra una Verga. Rappresentò degnamente questo sogetto chi fece Nettuno. S'aperse il Cielo, e in un sfondro luminosissimo, assisi in un maestoso Trono, si videro Giove, e Giunone. Era Giove coperto d'un manto stellato; sosteneva la chioma una corona di raggi, e la destra un fulmine. Rappresentò celestemente questa Deità chi fece Protheo. Quì per fine dell' Atto si cantò prima di dentro un altro Madrigale à più voci, concertato con Istrumenti diversi; E poi dodici Selvaggi uscirono à fare, per Intermezzo, un stravagantissimo, e gustosissimo ballo di moti, e gesti. Non vi fù occhio, che non lagrimasse il transito di questa danza. Ne fù l'Inventore il Signor Gio: Battista Balbi Ballarino sudetto. Si cambiò la Scena in Maritima; A tempo d'una dolcissima armonia, d'Istrumenti diversi comparve da un lato, della Scena una bellissima machina con Astrea, e Venere su. Volgevasi al destro ed' al sinistro late, come più à quelle Deità aggradiva. Le vicì à dirimpetto Mercurio; e aprendosi il Cielo assistè Giove nel mezzo. Fece un maraviglioso effetto questo Scenone, per la quantità delle machine, e per lo successivo ordine, della comparsa, e della gita. In un baleno divenne la Scena maritima un superbo Palagio. Fù bello, e caro il vedere da rozzi sassi, e da spiagge incolte nascere d'improviso un ben disegnato, e construto Edifitio. Figurava questi la Reggia d'Andromeda dalla quale uscì Ascalà Cavaliere. L'abito di costui eccedè di valuta, e di bellezza quello d'ogn' altro. Comparve vestito all' usanza Turca. Con mille gratie di Paradiso rappresentò questo dolente Personaggio chi fece Mercurio. Di repente sparito il Palagio, si vide la Scena tutta Mare con Andromeda legata ad' un sasso. Uscì 'l Mostro marino. Era con si bello artifitio fabricato quest' Animale, che ancorche non vero, pur metteva terrore. Tranne l'effetto di sbranare, e divorare, havea tutto di vivo, e di spirante. Venne Perseo dal Cielo sù'l Pegaseo, e con tre colpi, di lancea, e cinque di stocco fece l'abbattemento col Mostro, e l'uccise. Era questo Personaggio d'armibianche vestito, con un gran cimiero sù l'Elmo; e una Pennacchiera all' istessa divisa haveva il volante Destriere sù la fronte. Fù rappresentato questo sogetto angelicamente da chi fece Ascalà. S'aperce il Cielo, e si videro Giove, e Giunone in gloria, e altre Deità. Scese queste gran machinone in terra, accompagnato da un Concerto di voci, e di stromenti veramente di Paradiso. Levati i duo Heroi, che fra' di loro compli vano gli condusse al Cielo. Qui la regale, e sempre degna funtione hebbe fine.

APPENDIX IV
Casts for Operas in Venice before 1700
Marciana, Venice, MS.

The manuscript papers belonging to Francesco Caffi in the Marciana contain notes for a projected *Storia della Musica Teatrale in Venezia* from which this list of singers is taken. It is a supplement to the list published by me in *Music and Letters*, vol. xxx, April 1949. 'Some Early Venetian Opera Productions.'

Date: 1648; Theatre: S. Cass.; Title: *Torilda*; Composer: Fr. Cavalli; Author: Conte Pierpaolo Bisarri; Cast:

Anna Renzi, Romana	Giambatista Meggiorana
Anna Maria Ferrari	Girolamo Autignati
Cecilia Scutari	

Date: 1649; Theatre: SS. G. e P.; Title: *Argiope*; Composers: Rovetta, Leardini; Author: G. B. Fusconi; Cast: Anna Renzi.

Date: 1655; Theatre: S. Salv.; Title: *Erismena*; Composer: Cavalli; Author: Aureli; Cast: Caterina Porri, Romana.

Date: 1673; Theatre: S. Moisè; Title: *La Costanza Trionfante*; Composer: Giandomenico Partenio; Author: Ivanovich; Cast:

Teresa Bolsani	Sebastiano Rosa m
Orsola Parmeni	Pietro Corte
Carlo Lesma	Sebastiano Orfei m (da donna)
Giovanni Carletti m[1]	Antonio Cola

Date: 1678–90; Theatre: S. G. Gr.; Title: *Vespasiano*; Composer: C. Pallavicino; Author: G. C. Corradi; Cast:

Giulia Zuffi	Marcantonio Orrigoni
Francesca Cottini	Francesconieria Sassi m
Basso Salina	Alessandro Moscaner
Francesco Grossi m	Tommaso Boni (parte buffa)

Date: 1679; Theatre: S. G. Gr.; Title: *Nerone*; Composer: C. Pallavicino; Author: G. C. Corradi; Cast:

Maria Giuseppe	Francesco de Castris
Gianfranco Grossi m	Filippo Rustichelli
Antonio Coresi m (da donna)	Tommaso Boni

Date: 1680; Theatre: S. G. Gr.; Title: *Vespasiano*; Composer: C. Pallavicino; Author: G. C. Corradi; Cast:

Caterina Angiola Boteghi	Alessandro Girardini
Anna Maria Scalati [*sic*][2]	Francesco Ballarini
Antonio Formenti	Francesco de Castris m (da donna)
Francesco Grossi	Tommaso Boni
Giuseppemaria Donati	

[1] 'Musico', a term used to denote a castrato.   [Scarlattis', *M.R.* 1951.
[2] Cf. Edward Dent, *Alessandro Scarlatti*, pp. 36–37 and Frank Walker, 'Some Notes on the

Date: 1680; Theatre: S. G. Gr.; Title: *Il Ratto delle Sabine*; Composer: Cav. P. S. Angiolini; Author: G. Bissari; Cast as above.

Date: 1682; Theatre: S. G. Gr.; Title: *Flavio Cuniberto*; Composer: Pietro Partenio; Author: M. Noris; Cast:

Donne, Lucrezia Fichiboni
    Margerita Salicola
    Clarice Gigli
Uomini, Domenico Cecchi detto Cortona m

Uomini, Giuseppe Canovase
    Antonio Formenti ten
    Francesco de Castris m
    Tommaso Boni buffa

Date: 1682; Theatre: S. G. Gr.; Title: *Carlo Re d'Italia*; Composer: C. Pallavicino; Author: M. Noris; Cast as above and:

Annamaria Manarin

Margerita Salicola (da donne)

Date: 1683; Theatre: S. G. Gr.; Title: *Il Re Infante*; Composer: C. Pallavicino; Author: M. Noris; Cast:

Margherita Salicola[1]
Antonia Marzori
Clarice Gigli
Carlantonio Zata m
Francesco Ballarini m

Gianfrancesco Grossi m
Antonio Formenti
Giovanni Buzzoleni
Pierpaolo Scandalibene
Tommaso Boni buffo

Date: 1684; Theatre: S. G. Gr.; Title: *Licenio imperatore*; Composer: C. Pallavicino; Author: M. Noris; Cast:

Margarita Salicola
Clarice Gigli
Domenico Cecchi detto Cortona m
Francesco de Castris m

Giuseppe Canavase ten
Francesco Ballarini
D. Tommaso Boni
Antonio Formenti ten

Date: 1687; Theatre: S. G. Gr.; Title: *Elmiro Re di Corinto*; Composer: C. Pallavicino; Author: [V. Grimani]; Cast:

Caterina Durò

D. Tommaso Boni

Date: 1688; Theatre: S. G. Gr.; Title: *Orazio*; Composer: G. F. Tosi; Author: Nob. Ven. V. Grimani; Cast:

Vittoria Bombaci
Laura Spade
un basso di Polonia
Giacomo Filippo Cabella

un Padre Servità
D. Tommaso Boni
Nicola Tricarico
Alessandro Girardini m

[1] *Mercure Galant*, March 1683: 'Elle est blonde, de taille mediocre, et le teint fort blanc, beaucoup de brillant, une maniere libre et aisée, l'air de qualité, et est une bonne Comédienne.'

Date: 1688; Theatre: S. G. Gr.; Title: *Carlo il Grande*; Composer: D. Gabrieli;
Author: Morselli; Cast:

Vittoria Bombaci	un Padre Servità
Laura Spada	Alessandro Girardini m
Angiola Gringher	Faustino Marchesi m
Giacomo Filippo Cabella	un basso di Polonia
Nicola Tricarico	Tommaso Boni

Date: 1689; Theatre: SS. Gio. e P.; Title: *Il Gran Tamerlano*; Composer: M. A.
Ziani; Author: G. C. Corradi; Cast:

Annamaria Torri	Pierpaolo Scandalimbeni ten
Elena Cavazzoni	Lorenzo Sartini, da Fabriano m
Giuseppe Segni di Finale m	Giovanni Rosetto, Veneziano
Giuseppe Scaccia	

Date: 1689; Theatre: S. G. Gr.; Title: *Armilio e Numitore*; Composer: G. F. Tosi;
Author: Morselli; Cast:

Anna Maria Lisa	Antonfrancesco Carli ten
Angiola Gringher	D. Tommaso Boni
Francesco de Grandis m	

Date: 1690; Theatre: S. Salv.; Title: *Brenno in Efeso*; Composer: G. A. Perti;
Author: A. Arcoleo; Cast:

Angelica Zannoni	Pietro Mozzi
Clarice Venturini di Parma	Francesco Grandis ten di Spagna
Elena Cavazzoni di Parma	Antonio Panconi, Fiorentino m
Francesco Ballerini ten di Mantova	Valentino Urbani, Udinese

Date: 1690; Theatre: S. G. Gr.; Title: *Pirro e Demetrio*; Composer: G. Tosi;
Author: Morselli; Cast:

Faustina Periagini, Romana	Faustino Marchesi m, Modena
Diana Testi, Mantova	Ferdinando Chiaravalle, Mantova
Francesco Pistocchi m, Parma	Tommaso Boni
Giovanni Buzzoleni ten, Mantova	

Date: 1691; Theatre: Ai Saloni; Title: *Gli amori fortunati negli equivoci*; Cast:

Olimpia Manucci, Romana	Antonio Girardini, Padovano
Domenica Augusti, Veneziana	Michelangelo Gasperini, m

Date: 1691; Theatre: S. G. Gr.; Title: *La Pace fra Tolommio e Selenco*; Composer:
C. F. Pollaroli; Author: Morselli; Cast:

Laura Spada (da uomo)	Giordano, Turinese
Diana Testi	Francesco Pistocchi m
Orelli Diana, Turinese	Romolo Ferini
Giovanni Buzzoleni	Tommaso Boni

Date: 1691; Theatre: S. G. Gr.; Title: *L'Incoronazione di Serse*; Composer: Felice Tosi; Author: Morselli; Cast:

Diani Testi	Giordano Turinese
Orelli Diana Turinese	Antonio Romolo Ferini
Francesco Pistocchi m	Tommaso Boni
Giovanni Buzzoleni	

Date: 1691; Theatre: S. Salv.; Title: *La Virtù Trionfante*; Composer: M. A. Ziani; Author: Silvani; pitt. scenico Carlo Basso.

Date: 1692; Theatre: S. G. Gr.; Title: *Onorio in Roma*; Composer: G. F. Pollarolo; Author: Giannini; Cast:

Orette Diana Turinese	Pietro Moggi ten
Lucrezia Trombettina	Giansecondo Ofelio
Francesco Pistocchi m	Romolo Fareni
	Tommaso Boni

Quest' Opera fu resa harmoniosa dal Sig. Carlo Pollaroli in poco più d'una settimana: non dico favola. E dunque anzi probabile che non sarà state molto armoniosa.

Date: 1692; Theatre: S. G. Gr.; Title: *Ifraim Sultano*; Composer: C. F. Pollaroli; Author: Morselli; Cast:

Orette Diana Turinese	Antonio Romolo Ferini
Lucrezia Trombettina	Pietro Moggi ten
Giansecondo Ofelia	D. Tommaso Boni
Francesco Pistocchi m	

Date: 1693; Theatre: S. G. Gr.; Title: *La Forza della Virtù*; Composer: C. F. Pollaroli; Author: Domenico David; Cast:

Vittoria Tarquinii	Vincenzo Dati
Domenica Pini	Pietro Moggi
Giovanni Bruzzoleni ten	Tommaso Boni
Antonio Romolo Ferini m	

Date: 1694; Theatre: S. G. Gr.; Title: *Ottone*; Composer: C. F. Pollaroli; Author: Conte Girol° Frigimelica Roberti; Cast:

Angiola Gringher	Giulio Cavaletti
Antonia Marzari	Nicola Tricarico
Giulia Marzari	Pietro Moggi
Francesco Ballarini	Tommaso Boni

Date: 1695; Theatre: S. G. Gr.; Title: *Il Pastore d'Anfriso*; Composer: C. F. Pollaroli; Author: Conte Girol° Frigimelica Roberti; Cast:

Antonia Margari	Vincenzo Dati
Diamante Maria Scarabelli	Giacomo Filippo Cabella ten
Valentino Urbani m	Tommaso Boni
Francesco Ballarini m	

Date: 1695; Theatre: S. G. Gr.; Title: *Irene*; Composer: [C. F. Pollaroli]; Author: Conte Girol° Frigimelica Roberti; Cast: as above.

Date: 1696; Theatre: S. Cass.; Title: *Clotilde*; Composer: Gianmaria Ruggeri; Author: [Giovanni Battista Neri]; pitt. scenici Lorenzo Domenichino.

Date: 1696; Theatre: S. Salv.; Title: *La finta pazzia d'Ulisse*; Composer: M. A. Ziani; Author: M. Noris; pitt. scenico Ferdinando Bibiena.

Date: 1696; Theatre: S. Cass.; Title: *Basilio re d'Oriente*; Composer: Fr. Navarra; Author: D. Giambatista Neri; pitt. scenici Lorenzo Domenichino.

Date: 1696; Theatre: S. G. Gr.; Title: *Rosimonda*; Composer: C. F. Pollaroli; Author: G. F. Roberti; Cast:

Maria Landini	Pierpaolo Scandalibene
Diana Averara	Nicola Paris m
due giovanni dette le Polacchini	Francesco Ballarini
Tasi —	Tommaso Boni
Biretta —	

Date: 1696; Theatre: S. G. Gr.; Title: *Ercole in cielo*; Composer: C. F. Pollaroli; Author: Conte G. F. Roberti; Cast: as above.

Date: 1697; Theatre: S. G. Gr.; Title: *Tito Manlio*; Composer: C. F. Pollaroli; Author: M. Noris; Cast:

Angiola Gringher	Antonio Romolo Ferini
Maria Domenica Pini	Michelangelo Gasparini m
Anton Francesco Carli	Tommaso Boni
Matteo Sappani m	

Date: 1697; Theatre: S. G. Gr.; Title: *Amor e Dovere*; Composer: C. F. Pollaroli; Author: Domenico David; Cast: as above.

Date: 1698; Theatre: S. G. Gr.; Title: *Tito Manlio* [repetition]; Cast:

Francesca Vanini	Luigi Morelli
Lucrezia Carò	Michelangelo Gasparini
Anton Francesco Carli ten	Tommaso Boni
Domenico Cecchi detto Cortona m	

Date: 1698; Theatre: S. G. Gr.; Title: *Marzio Coriolano*; Composer: C. F. Pollaroli; Author: M. Noris; Cast:

Lucrezia Carò	Luigi Morelli
Francesca Vanini Boschi	Giansecondo Orselia
Antonfrancesco Carli ten	Tommaso Boni
Domenico Cecchi detto Cortona m	

Date: 1699; Theatre: S. Salv.; Title: *Amor per Virtù*; Composer: Antonio Draghi;
Author: Domenico Cupeda; Cast:

Annamaria Battaglia, Bolognese	Filippo Sandri, Veronese
Margherita Raimondi, Veronese	Carlo Campelli
Oliviero Matraja	Paolo Teodorovich di Osimo

Date: 1699; Theatre: S. G. Gr.; Title: *Faramondo*; Composer: C. F. Pollaroli;
Author: Apostolo Zeno; Cast:

Maria Domenica Pini	Michelangelo Gasparini m
Lucrezia Carò	Giovanni Archi
Francesca Dupina (da uomo)	Francescantonio Pistocchi m
Antonfrancesca Carli ten	Giambatista Franceschini m

Date: 1699; Theatre: S. G. Gr.; Title: *Il ripudio d'Ottavia*; Composer: C. F. Pollaroli; Author: M. Noris; Cast:

Maria Domenica Pini	Giambatista Franceschini
Annamaria Torri	Giannantonio Archi (da donna) m
Francesca Dupina da uomo	Michelangelo Gasparini m
Francescantonio Pistocchi m	Tommaso Boni.
Antonfrancesco Carli ten	

Il Bellerofonte

A musical drama by Vicenzo Nolfi given in the Novissimo theatre in Venice by Giacomo Torelli of Fano, the inventor of the machines. Dedicated to Ferdinand II, Grand Duke of Tuscany, 1642

The author of the work to the reader.

You waste time, O reader, if, with the poetics of the Stagirite in hand, you go seeking out the errors of this work. For I freely confess that in its composition I have not wished to observe other precepts than the sentiments of the inventor of the apparatus. Nor have I a higher aim than the Genius of that people for whom it is shown.

This is the type of poetry which returns to the first nature of Drama as much as Song and is reduced as much to a different culture as the taste of the century demands, the wits of our time not recognizing to-day Epicarme for father, nor Sicily as fatherland nor Aristotle as law-giver any more.

All customs change and Novelty pleases as well as corrupts as Scaliger says of the Amphitryon of Plautus.

If any Crates', Aristophanes' and Terences were alive to-day, their thoughts would be different perhaps.

Of the two ends for Poetry taught by Horace there only remains to delight. In this age men have no need to learn the life of the world from the other compositions.

But the point is that not even this will be found in these pages since the story, ruined from the Ancients, has been renovated by my pen in Dramatic shape in the briefest of short times in order to receive the beauty of the machines and theatrical apparatus. And here is this dead body renewed to life by means of those spirits born in the sweetness and artifice of the music composed by Sign. Francesco Sacrati of Parma with the harmonious voices of the most celebrated singers of Europe. Go to the New Theatre. There you will see what you have needed.

Extracts from the description of the production written by Giulio del Colle.

Prologue. The curtain rises quickly to discover the Scene representing the port of the city of Patera. On the left along the mole, lie many ships of Anthea, many, having just arrived, with sails not entirely furled and gilded prows and standards of various colours unfurled in the air. On the right, in good order, are the turreted walls of the city not sufficiently high to prevent the summits of the highest buildings within the city from appearing. The sea runs obliquely from left to right kissing the last wall and extending behind in perspective with two towers in the distance guarding the entrance of the mole. Farther off there was nothing more to hinder the eye, in case it might not wander over the vastness of the water with delicious conceit. It was so perfect, as in all the other things portrayed, that, however much I may sing in praise

PLATE 12

Il
Bellero Fonte
Drama Musicale Del Sig^r
Vicenzo Nolfi da F.
Rappresentato Nel Teatro
Novissimo in Venetia
Da Giacomo
Torelli Da Fano Inventore
delli Apparati
1642.

PLATE 13

Il Bellerofonte, Act I. 3

PLATE 14

a. Il Bellerofonte, Act I. 3

b. Il Bellerofonte, Act I. 11

primarily of the inventor and then of the painter, it would be always much less than they deserve.

In mid stage is seen Innocence fittingly played by a soprano from Parma dressed in white (con habito di ornesino bianco) trimmed with gold with a very beautiful head-dress and a long cloak of cloth of gold worn in a stately manner.

A shining machine appeared, as if touched with gold, out of a few rent-opened clouds, made with singular art. And, breaking away completely from the sky, it came to the ground without permitting the eye to penetrate to its supports. Upon it sat Justice with a Lion and, by her side, a sword, scales in her hand, clothed in a blue coat sprinkled with gold, rich and beautiful above manner. A valorous castrato from Rome took the part who gained great applause for noble and stately gestures in a noteworthy performance.

Then, from the right of the sea, arose a car in the form of a golden shell drawn by sea-horses which moved from the right to the centre of the stage, turned round and stopped facing the body of the theatre. This car bore Neptune king of the waves, surrounded by his Tritons, excellently played. He was entirely naked except for a beautiful rich blue and gold cloak which covered him in some parts. A tenor from Parma took the part gaining praise and giving wonderful satisfaction to the audience.

At his command a most exquisite and life-like model of Venice arose from the sea which everyone confessed to be a *tour de force*. The eye was deceived by the Piazza and public buildings which were imitated to the life and it rejoiced more hourly as it forgot that the entertainment came from a concealment of the truth. . . .

The prologue, a great pledge and trial of the whole drama being finished, six soldiers, eight halberdiers and four pages of King Ariobarte, servants of his chief captain Paristide, came from the principal gate of the city in long file and went toward the pier to meet his daughter the widowed Queen of Argos. The soldiers were armed with cuirasses and helmets with blue plumes. They wore blue stockings, a livery trimmed with great golden roses, skirts of gold lace, sashes of blue and gold crepe from which hung their swords, and gold buskins on their feet. Their captain wore rich armour encrusted with jewels, a blue sash, plume and smart looking half-boots. The halberdiers were dressed as janissaries with undercoats of red and gold with surcoats of blue to their feet with ruffles, great collars in the Greek style, lined with beautifully coloured cloth, trimmed with gold, and janissary berets with falling plumes matching the surcoats. Sashes of cloth of gold held their scimitars. And in their hands they bore very evil lances. The pages were dressed entirely in silver, full breeches (bragoni interi) half-boots and Polish berets with silver plumes. On their shoulders they had coats open at the neck in front, with half-sleeves, blue at the sides and lined with cloth of red and gold with gold lacings. These *comparse* gave amazing pleasure. And the audience admitted that a royal court could not have arranged it with greater propriety and beauty. The clothes worn by Paristides were very grand. The part was taken by a tenor from Pistoia with a very sweet voice. The king wore a coat of gold brocade down to his knees, with a superb royal cloak lined with gold and an ermine collar. He carried a jewelled sceptre and, on his head, above a beautiful turban, he wore a golden crown. The part was played by a bass from Siena who deserved praise throughout the piece.

The first *comparse* were still on the stage when the ships at the shore put out bridges to be used by Anthea's court who came out, consisting of six soldiers under a chief, four pages, six ladies and the nurse Delfiride. There was no difference between these soldiers and those of the king except that these wore black and silver; likewise the pages wore black and silver livery. The ladies had black and silver coats trimmed with silver lace above which they had a little surcoat of black cloth and silver lace which was very beautiful to behold. Partly covered by this coat was a golden stomacher powdered with red and opened at the breasts which puffed the material. In addition they wore capes of the same cloth that hung down to their feet, jewels and pearls on their necks and bosoms.

The Queen entered dressed in a coat entirely of gold covered by a most cunning black veil and a long rich cloak, a crown on her head and a jewelled sceptre in her right hand. There is no need to write of the qualities of Signora Giulia Sans Paolelli of Rome who played the Queen. For during the three years during which she has honoured this town by her presence, her talents have become known. . . . Delfiride, the nurse, attended her, dressed in a black coat and long veil ('bende'). The part was taken by a castrato from Parma, highly esteemed ('d'alta virtù') who played so true to life that, above all the others, he drew the most individual applause. . . .

Scene 3.

To succeed these personages as they left there was the delight of a few clouds which appeared in mid-air. Upon one sat Pallas and the goddess Diana, guardian of Bellerophon a hero by his wisdom, strength and chastity. For he was directly taught by these divinities and noble above all others. Pallas wore a shining cuirass and helmet, a petticoat of blue and gold, rich with jewels, white rings and necklace. And she carried a lance and shield with the Gorgon's head. Diana's coat was white, embroidered with gold with a short surcoat of gold sprinkled within with countless jewels: a little half-moon on her head, a bow in her hand and quiver at her side. The two worthies were castrato sopranos who played their parts perfectly. The machine descended in one piece for a little way and then divided. Slowly descending, the two clouds bore the goddesses to the ground on either side of the stage, with a movement both unexpected and marvellous, without showing how it was arranged, and straightway scattered, through the scene ('e rette disperdendosi per il palco') without the means being understood by the amazed audience.

Up till now the eye had rejoiced in the sight of the artificial port and seaboard which in one moment astonished beyond all thought by the speed with which they were timed and arranged (mossi, e condotti confusero con la velocità, e unione fin il pensiero). The cunning of the great wheel, to every movement of which the flats responded immediately, could be likened to the egg of a pigeon (l'arteficio della gran ruota cui ubbidiscono a un tempo i mote d'ogni telaro l'uovo del colombo non senza ragione chiamar si puote): for, in general, it set aside every little mechanism previously well known. It had never been used before excepting, after practice, in the Teatro Novissimo last year. Now the scene represented a royal courtyard, made stately and pompous by a very long row of pilasters, little windows, doors and statues exquisitely measured and artistically arranged. The perspective of doric and rustic architecture, like the courtyard, formed a great theatre. At its side two stair-cases ascended to the top. Facing was an open door through which were arranged rows of cypress trees leading to a view of a beautiful garden. First to appear on this scene was a lady of the court, Melista, played by a very worthy castrato from Pistoia, clad with rich abandon in a well-thought-out dress in Greek style of gold brocade with the correct adornments on his head which gave peculiar satisfaction.

Scene 11.

Now the courtyard disappeared with unexpected speed. The whole sky, an in-expressible wonder, represented the grotto of the winds of Eolus as described by the ancient story-tellers. In several places there were clefts, and, facing, the ruins of the cavern did not hide the view of the distant sea. Eolus, king of the winds, singularly played by a Siennese bass entered with his wife Anfitea in order to loose his enchained vassals to help his nephew Bellerophon. He was dressed in a breastplate of gold almost entirely sprinkled with rubies as roses. His girdle and mantle were of blue and gold cloth. He was proud and stately with a crown on his head and a bridle in his hands. His wife was dressed in a long black garment but entirely embroidered in silver above which she had a smaller garment with golden patterns powdered with green and a rich cloak of black and silver.

At his first commands some rocks fell and behind them, as if chained, were Winds, four at the sides and others facing. They were naked except for half-boots; some stuffs of silver flowing and fluttering from their shoulders and girdles of gold. For the rest they had those masks of which poets speak. After the king had spoken liberating them, two at the side rose quickly into the air and in one straight move-ment flew obliquely to the opposite side. The other two then disappeared to the side. Of those facing, three simultaneously flew into mid-air and then divided in a marvellous way. The last one plunged below ground and in his violence almost dis-turbed the dark depths of the sea. And with this marvellous spectacle, and with machines so strange for their speed, balance, and extravagance of movement the first Act of the drama came to an end. And the swans of the theatre were enabled to have a little rest from so many wonders.

Act II. 1.

At the opening of the second Act, by an unexpected change of scene, instead of the grotto, in a moment there is the uninhabited island of Magistea, the horrid nest of the Chimera. It looked wooded with a few buildings which were seen to be ruins inside and falling to bits. However these ruins were charming and full of artifice. And the condition of the wood in which each tree was carved with individual care was no less worthy of note in its design and painting. Facing, the waves of a great sea were rolling, and behind it, in a distant perspective, was the city of Patera, on the sands of Licia, exquisitely fashioned with well-arranged lighting. Diana and Minerva, guardian deities of Bellerophon entered from the town, assisted by a knight and prepared for battle. . . . At the withdrawal of the Goddess, Bellerophon was seen riding Pegasus in the air. He was Signor Michiele Grasseschi a contralto to the Serene Prince Matthias of Tuscany who can never be sufficiently praised. He flew slowly across from left to right and turned towards the centre of the stage where, with terrible leapings and boundings the Chimera was searching for him. The hero wounded it with an arrow. And it turned towards the horse, attacking in great leaps and spitting flame from its mouth. At this Pegasus flew in a straight line across to the edge of the scene up to the architrave. And here, once more, Bellerophon turning again shot it. He then flew swiftly to the left of the stage in an oblique line whence he shot his third arrow. Lastly he sent another from the right whither he had gone at the same speed. The very savage monster who was always running in the tracks of his foe seemed then to lose strength. Therefore Pegasus descended to earth very quickly. Bellerophon dismounted and cut off the heel of the suffering Chimera. When he remounted, the horse turned to the other side and flew up high disappearing in the clouds. This machine was worth remembering and not easily imitated. From it the inventor had, and always will have, particular praise.

Scene 3.

At the invocation of the two goddesses, clouds drifted in from all sides, splitting open in the centre to give a view of a golden palace studded with jewels in Doric, Ionic and Roman architecture. It had, in front, a roofed courtyard with steps at the sides and long rows of columns that seemed to support, under plain arches, a construction of great height. Farther off in good perspective a loggia was displayed, behind which were views of rooms with, in the centre, staircases on either side. These led to the upper row where there appeared superbly, above the arches and not hidden by clouds, a great chamber, and other rooms. Beneath the first entrance was Venus, on her car drawn by doves, with her little son Amore as coachman. The car was gilt and spattered (tempestato) with jewels. Two *amorini* behind held the golden apple, the favourite device of that goddess. It was wonderful to see this car mount into the air in a moment and turn straight towards the bottom of the scene (front of the stage). When the deities had descended, the car without showing any of the mechanism moved to the other side. When this machine was again reloaded as before, Minerva and Diana mounted their own little clouds and, simultaneously all the machines rose and hid themselves in the sky. These sights indeed, could not have been shown in a more unique and majestic spectacle.

Scene 4.

Now the island and sea disappeared and the scene opened with a delicious garden in the kingdom of Ariobate. In it were well-arranged espaliers of orange trees, limes, and jessamines which appeared to lean against different buildings and pleasure-houses with low balustrades, which supported statues here and vases there of excellent imitation flowers. In the far perspective, beneath a vault of greenery and upheld by four great posts, sat a Neptune on a dolphin from whose mouth appeared

PLATE 15

a. Il Bellerofonte, Act II. 1

b. Il Bellerofonte, Act II. 3

PLATE 16

a. Il Bellerofonte, Act II. 4

b. Il Bellerofonte, Act II. 11

to issue a large volume of water collecting into a great vase of singular artifice. The vista continued and one soon lost oneself in a long avenue of cypress trees forming a wonderful view.

This scene also did not lack beauty since Anthea and Delfiride her nurse shone in it. Amore made an entry, flying from the left with great speed to the middle of the scene. He wounded the former. Then, rising again, he flew to the right drawing the eyes of the theatre who, astonished, tried in vain to penetrate the machinery and discover the artifice.

Scene 11.

Here the garden scene became a temple the courtyard of which was decorated with beautiful porticos and twisted columns bound with roses and fluted in a very lovely fashion. Above this row was a balustrade with bases and imitation capitals of gold. The perspective of the same type was separated in such a way that another view of arches could be seen upheld by straight Roman pillars and a very superb ceiling, above it a portico or passage which joined the sides all quite separate. Within the temple there was a long row of arches and pilasters at the end of which doors opened as exits. In the middle was set an altar upon which stood a statue of Giove adored by the ancients. I believe it impossible to excel or indeed to equal the nobility and majesty of this scene. And the most intelligent architects and painters had, in seeing it, something to wonder at. For all that was perfect was fulfilled in it. And more, this scene was enriched by all the 'extras' of the opera. King Ariobate, his two children entered at once, and Bellerophon to present the head of the Chimera and to give thanks to the Gods for the liberation of the kingdom from the scourge. To meet them came out a proper chorus of priests with their principal, clothed in shirts of silver stuff flowered in different colours with short over-garments of a kind of damask embroidered with gold and with silver mitres on their heads. The principal was clad with greater pomp. His clothes of gold brocade made him more noteworthy and majestic than the others.

The second Act finished by a withdrawal of these personages. And the theatre awaited with impatience the third act in which, from the things already seen, they were certain would be brought anew contrivances always more rare.

Act III. 1.

At the beginning of the third Act the temple had disappeared and the scene became a delicious and well set out grove in the royal gardens in which Nature came to acknowledge herself overcome by a rival Art, so well arranged and imitated were the trees and so well portrayed to the life was the deliciously horrid spot (dilettosa horridezza) from which no one's passions could discover a way out. And the theatre seemed, like a new Serse, to take and make love to the plants. Facing, three arches were made by twisted trunks of laurel beyond which stretched long avenues of cypress and palm which ran into a point leading, at the extreme distance, to the royal palace. In this set were two *amorini*, the one wanton and the other chaste. These two, after plotting over the affections of Anthea, took to the air in a wonderful flight, one, in a very nimble transverse movement, hid himself in the clouds, the other rose slowly at first to the middle of the sky then, very swiftly, passed from the left to the right of the stage. Later, in another almost instantaneous flight, he dropped a little to earth then bore himself up to the sky. Sufficient has been said about the machines and inventions but always less than they deserved. And here, whilst praise remains as usual weak, it were useless to increase it except to testify to the unique difficulty of these operations which another expert has probably encountered in hazarding similar scenes.

Scene 8.

Up to this point indeed, the scene appeared exquisite and costly but it consisted in the improvement and increase of the general theatrical practice, in courtyards, gardens and suchlike. But here the change was unique and novel, no longer in the accustomed practice. Numerous and large flats issued from the wings both at the sides and from above which carried others with them. Out of them a royal room was made with, facing, flat arches upheld by columns, with composite counter pilasters and architecture, ornaments and cornices. These were joined by hangings of red and yellow damask as was, or appeared to be, the whole room, except where the set was broken by doors through which, with the door-curtains lifted, the eye was carried deeper within. The ceiling, which reached right under the proscenium arch, was made to look like beams worked with golden arabesques of extraordinary cunning (Era il soffitto, che arrivava fin sotto l'arco della Scena finto a travatura di noce lavorata a rabeschi d'oro con sopraordinerio artificio). But there were greater discoveries for, shortly, curtains were drawn showing five more arches, following the order of the others, which upheld a lower ceiling quite different from the first, made separately and worked beautifully in squares. This great chamber was decorated with the same finery as the room. And, at the back, was an exit which had, on either side, doors from the side rooms separated by their own arches, leading finally, by a cypress avenue, to the royal garden. Beside the main arch of the exit were two doors leading to another three which ultimately passed into the same avenue and garden. These were hung with different-coloured tapestries, green, red and yellow with such noble harmony and dignity throughout, and with such rare and marvellous invention that the inventor will be able to be glorious for all time.

In this scene Archimene, the royal daughter, was played by Signora Anna Renzi, a Roman, the absolute and amazingly unique ideal of a musician. During the course of the plot, although on occasions she became a woman of normal humour and feeling, she eventually gained her beloved Bellerophon for husband, declaiming, feigning and grieving with lover's passions. And as a perfection and sign of their glory her sister Anthea was seen to yield up the crown of her own will with which action, to a thousand voices of applause, the present drama closed.

PLATE 17

a. Il Bellerofonte, Act III. 1

b. Il Bellerofonte, Act III. 8

PLATE 18

Apparati Scenici
Per lo Teatro Novissimo di Venetia.
Nell' anno 1644
d'inventione e cura
di
Jacomo Terelli Da Fano

PLATE 19

a

b

Apparati Scenici

PLATE 20

a

b

Apparati Scenici

PLATE 21

a

b

Apparati Scenici

PLATE 22

a

b

Apparati Scenici

PLATE 23

a

b

Apparati Scenici

Bibliography

ABBREVIATIONS

DdT	*Denkmäler deutscher Tonkunst.*	PMA	*Proceedings of the Musical Association.*
DTB	*Denkmäler der Tonkunst in Bayern.*		
DTOe	*Denkmäler der Tonkunst in Oester-reich.*	Rass M	*La Rassegna musicale.*
		RHCM	*Revue d'histoire et de critique musicales.*
JMP	*Jahrbuch der Musikbibliothek Peters.*		
		RM	*Revue musicale.*
MfMg	*Monatshefter für Musikgeschichte.*	RMI	*Rivista Musicale italiana.*
M & L	*Music and Letters.*	SIMG	*Sammelbände der internationalen Musikgesellschaft.*
MM	*Mercure musical.*		
MQ	*Musical Quarterly.*	SzMw	*Studien zur Musikwissenschaft.*
MTNA	*Proceedings of the Music Teachers' National Association.*	VfMw	*Vierteljahrsschrift für Musikwissenschaft.*

ALLACCI, A. *Drammaturgia . . . accresciuta e continuata fino all' anno MDCCLV.* (Venice) 1755.

BEARE, M. *The German Popular Play Atis and the Venetian Opera: a Study of the Conversion of Operas into Popular Plays 1675–1722.* (Cambridge) 1938.

BELLONI, A. *Storia letteraria d'Italia: il Seicento.* (Milan) 1948.

BENVENUTI, G. 'Il manoscritto veneziano della *Incoronazione di Poppea*', RMI xli (1937).

BERGMANS, P. 'Une Collection de livrets d'opéras italiens (1669–1710)', M & L xvii (1936).

BONAVENTURA, A. *Saggio storico sul teatro musicale italiano.* (Leghorn) 1913.

BERLINER, R. *Chronicle of the Museum for the Arts of Decoration of the Cooper Union*, vol. i (1941).

BORREN, CH. VAN DEN. *Les Débuts de la musique à Venise.* (Brussels) 1914.

—— *Il ritorno d'Ulisse in patria di Claudio Monteverdi.* (Brussels) 1925.

BÜCKEN, E. *Der heroische Stil in der Oper.* (Leipzig) 1924.

BUKOFZER, M. *Music in the Baroque Era.* (London) 1948.

BUSTICO, G. 'Bibliografia delle storie e cronistorie dei teatri italiani', *Bollettino bibliografico musicale.* (Milan) 1929.

CAFFI, F. *Storia della Musica Sacra nella già Cappella Ducale di San Marco in Venezia.* 2 vols. (Venice) 1854.

CHAMPIGNEULLE, B. 'L'Influence de Lully hors de France', RM xxii (1946).

CHEVAILLIER, L. 'Le Récit chez Monteverdi', RHCM x (1910).

CORONELLI, P. *Guida de' Forestieri per succintamente osservare tutto il più riguardevole nella Città di Venetia.* (Venice) 1697.

D'ANCONA, A. *Origini del teatro italiano.* 2nd ed. 2 vols. (Turin) 1891.

D'ARIENZO, N. 'Le origini dell' opera comica', RM ii (1895); iv (1897); vi (1899); vii (1900).

DAVARI, S. 'Notizie biografiche del distinto maestro di musica Claudio Monteverdi', *Atti e memorie della R. Accademia Virgiliana di Mantova*, x (1884–5).

DELLA CORTE, A. 'Tragico e comico nell' opera veneziana della seconda parte del seicento', Rass M xi (1938).

DENT, E. J. *Alessandro Scarlatti, His Life and Works.* (London) 1904.

—— 'The Baroque Opera', *Musical Antiquary* (1909–10).

—— 'The Nomenclature of Opera', M & L xxv (1944).

DE PAOLI, D. *Claudio Monteverdi.* (Milan) 1945.

EVELYN, J. Memoirs, ed. Bray. 2 vols. (London) 1819.

FRATI, L. 'Per la storia della musica in Bologna nel secolo XVII', RMI xxxii (1925).

[GALVANI, T. N.] *I teatri musicali di Venezia nel secolo XVII.* (Milan) 1878.

GOLDSCHMIDT, H. 'Cavalli als dramatischer Komponist', MfMg xxv (1893).

—— 'Claudio Monteverdis Oper: *Il ritorno d'Ulisse in patria*', SIMG ix (1907–8).

—— *Die italienische Gesangsmethode des XVII. Jahrhunderts und ihre Bedeutung für die Gegenwart.* 2nd ed. (Breslau) 1892.

—— *Die Lehre von der vokalen Ornamentik, erster Band: das 17. und 18. Jahrhundert bis in die Zeit Glucks.* (Charlottenburg) 1907.

—— 'Monteverdi's *Ritorno d'Ulisse*', SIMG iv (1902–3).

—— *Studien zur Geschichte der italienischen Oper im 17. Jahrhundert.* 2 vols. (Leipzig) 1902. (Cf. review by R. Rolland, RHCM ii (1902).)

—— 'Zur Geschichte der Arien und Symphonie-Formen', MfMg xxxiii (1901).

GROPPO, A. *Catalogo di tutti i drammi per musica recitati ne' teatri di Venezia dall' anno 1637 sin all' anno presente 1745.* (Venice) [1745?].

GROUT, D. 'German Baroque Opera', MQ xxxii (1946).

—— 'The "Machine" Operas', *Bulletin of the Fogg Museum of Art, Harvard University,* ix, No. 5 (1941).

—— *A Short History of Opera.* 2 vols. (London) 1947.

HAAS, R. *Die Musik des Barocks.* (Potsdam) [1934].

GENTILI, A. 'La raccolta Mauro Foà nella Biblioteca Nazionale di Torino', RMI xxxiv (1927).

—— Stradella — *La Forza dell' Amor Paterno*, vocal score, ed. (trascritta e armonizzata) by A. Gentili, Ricordi (Milan) 1932.

HESS, H. *Zur Geschichte des Musikalischen Dramas im Seicento; die Opern Alessandro Stradellas.* (Leipzig) 1906.

HEUSS, A. 'Die venetianischen Opern-Sinfonien', SIMG iv (1903).

HJELMBORG, B. 'Une Partition de Cavalli', *Acta Musicologica,* xvi–xvii (1944–5).

IVANOVICH, C. *Poesie.* (Venice) 1673.

—— *Minerva al Tavolina.* (Venice) 1681, cont. 1688.

KINSKY, G. *A History of Music in Pictures.* (London) 1930.

KRETZSCHMAR, H. 'Monteverdi's *Incoronazione di Poppea*', VfMw x (1894).

—— 'Die venetianische Oper und die Werke Cavalli's und Cesti's', VfMw viii (1892).

—— *Geschichte der Oper.* (Leipzig) 1919.

LANG, P. H. *Music in Western Civilization.* (New York) 1941.

LECLERC, H. *Les Origines italiennes de l'architecture théâtrale moderne.* (Paris) 1946.

[LECLERCQ, L.] *Les Décors, les costumes, et la mise en scène au XVIIe siècle, 1615–1680, par Ludovic Celler.* (Paris) 1869.

LEICHTENTRITT, H. 'On the Prologue in Early Opera', MTNA xxxi (1936).

[LIMOJON DE ST. DIDIER, A.] *La Ville et la république de Venise.* (Paris) 1680.

LOEWENBERG, A. *Annals of Opera.* (Cambridge) 1943.

MALIPIERO, G. F. 'Claudio Monteverdi of Cremona', MQ xviii (1932).

MARIANI, V. 'Ricordando Sabbatini e Torelli scenografi marchigiani', *Rassegna Marchigiana,* xii (1934).

MAYLENDER, M. *Storia delle accademie d'Italia.* 5 vols. (Bologna) [1926–30].

Mercure Galant. (Paris) 1672–84.

MOLMENTI, P. *La storia di Venezia nella vita privata dalle origini alla caduta della repubblica.* 3 vols. (Bergamo) 1929.

—— 'Venezia nel Sec. XVII descritta da due contemporanei', *Emporium,* xlviii (Venice) 1918.

—— *Venezia alla metà del secolo XVII.* (Rome) 1916.

MONALDI, G. *Cantanti evirati celebri nel teatro italiano.* (Rome) 1920.

MOYNET, G. *La Machinerie théâtrale.* (Paris) 1893.

NANI, B. *Storia della repubblica Veneta.* (Venice) 1686.

NEUHAUS, M. 'Antonio Draghi', SzMw i (1913).

NOLHAC, P. and SOLERTI, A. *Il viaggio in Italia di Enrico III, re di Francia, e le feste a Venezia, Ferrara, Mantova, e Torino.* (Torino) 1890.

PAPADOPOLI, N. *Sul valore della moneta veneziana.* (Venice) 1885.

PRUNIÈRES, H. *Cavalli et l'opéra vénitien au XVIIe siècle.* (Paris) [1931].

—— *Claudio Monteverdi.* (Paris) 1924.

—— 'De l'interprétation des agréments du chant aux XVIIe et XVIIIe siècles', RM xiii (1932).

—— 'I libretti dell' opera veneziana nel secolo XVII', Rass M iii (1930).

—— 'Monteverdi's Venetian Operas', MQ x (1924).

—— 'Notes sur les origines de l'ouverture française', SIMG xii (1910–11).

—— *L'Opéra italien en France avant Lulli.* (Paris) 1913.

—— *La Vie et l'œuvre de Claudio Monteverdi.* 2nd ed. (Paris) 1931.

REDLICH, H. 'Notationsprobleme in Cl. Monteverdis *Incoronazione di Poppea*', *Acta Musicologica,* x (1938).

—— *Claudio Monteverdi—Life and Works.* (London) 1952.

RICCI, C. *Vita Barocca.* (Milan) 1904.

RICHARD, P. 'Stradella et les Contarini: épisode des mœurs vénitiennes au XVIIe siècle', *Le Ménestrel,* xxxii (1864–5); xxxiii (1865–6).

ROLLAND, R. 'Notes sur l'Orfeo de Luigi Rossi et sur les musiciens italiens à Paris, sous Mazarin', RHCM i (1901).

—— 'L'Opéra populaire à Venise: Francesco Cavalli', MM ii, No. i (1906).

—— *Les Origines du théâtre lyrique moderne; histoire de l'opéra en Europe avant Lully et Scarlatti.* New ed. (Paris) 1931.

RONCAGLIA, G. *La rivoluzione musicale italiana (secolo XVII).* (Milan) 1928.

ROSSI-DORIA, G. 'Opera', *Enciclopedia Italiana,* vol. xxv (1935).

SABBATINI, N. *Pratica di fabricar scene, e machine ne' teatri.* (Ravenna) 1638.

—— German ed., *Anleitung Dekorationen und Theatermaschinen herzustellen.* (Weimar) 1926.

—— French ed., *Pratique pour fabriquer scènes et machines de théâtre.* (Neuchâtel) 1942.

[SALVIOLI, G.] *I teatri musicali di Venezia nel secolo XVII.* (Milan) [1879].

SANDBERGER, A. 'Beziehungen der Königin Christine von Schweden zur italienischen Oper und Musik, insbesondere zu M. A. Cesti; mit einem Anhang über Cestis Innsbrucker Aufenthalt', *Bulletin de la Société union musicologique,* v (1925).

—— 'Zur venezianischen Oper', JMP xxxi (1924); xxxii (1925).

SANSOVINO, F. *Venetia. Città nobilissima con aggiunta da Giustiniano Martinioni.* (Venice) 1663.

SCHERILLO, M. 'La prima commedia musicale a Venezia', *Giornale storico della letteratura italiana,* i (1883).

SOLERTI, A. 'I rappresentazioni musicali di Venezia dal 1571 al 1605', RMI ix (1902)..

SONNECK, O. G. TH. *Catalogue of Opera Librettos printed before 1800.* Library of Congress (Washington) 1908.

STUART, R. L. 'Busenello's libretto to Monteverde's "L'incoronazione di Poppæa": its place in the history of the drama and the opera', *The Musical Times* (Oct. 1927).

—— 'Busenello's "L'incoronazione di Poppea" ', *Musical Opinion* (Jan. 1928).

TASSINI, G. *Curiosità Veneziane.* 6th ed. (Venice) 1933.

TESSIER, A. 'Giacomo Torelli a Parigi e la messa in scena delle Nozze di Peleo e Teti di Carlo Caproli', Rass M i (1928).

—— '*L'Orontée* de Lorenzani et l'*Orontea* du Padre Cesti', RM ix, No. 8 (1928).

—— 'La Décoration théâtrale à Venise', *La Revue de l'art ancien et moderne*, liv (1928).

TIBY, O. *L'Incoronazione di Poppea di Claudio Monteverdi.* (Florence) 1937.

TORCHI, L. 'L'accompagnamento degli istrumenti nei melodrammi italiani della prima metà del seicento', RMI i (1894); ii (1895).

—— 'Canzoni ed arie italiane ad una voce nel secolo XVII', RMI i (1894).

TORREFRANCA, F. 'Il "grande stregone" Giacomo Torelli e la scenografia del seicento', *Scenario* iii (1934).

TOWNELEY WORSTHORNE, S. P. 'Venetian theatres', M & L xxix (1948).

—— 'Some early Venetian opera productions', M & L xxx (1949).

VATIELLI, F. 'Operisti-librettisti dei secoli XVII e XVIII', RH xliii (1939).

VENICE. Calendar of State Papers, Venice.

—— I teatri di Venezia. (Milan) 1869.

—— 'La Scuola Veneziana (secolo XVI–XVIII)', *Accademia Musicale Chigiana* (Siena), 1941.

WELLESZ, E. 'Die Aussetzung des Basso Continuo in der italienischen Oper', *International Musical Society, Fourth Congress Report.* (London) 1912.

—— 'Cavalli und der Stil der venetianischen Oper von 1640–1660', SzMw i (1913).

—— 'Zwei Studien zur Geschichte der Oper im 17. Jahrhundert', SIMG xv (1913).

—— *Essays on Opera.* (London) 1950.

WESTRUP, J. 'Monteverde's "Poppæa" ', *The Musical Times* (Nov. 1927).

—— 'Monteverde's "Il Ritorno d'Ulisse in patria" ', *The Monthly Musical Record* (April 1928).

—— 'Stages in the history of opera I—Claudio Monteverde', *The Musical Times* (Aug. 1929).

—— 'The Originality of Monteverdi', PMA lx (1933–4).

—— 'Monteverdi and the Orchestra', M & L xxii (1940).

WIEL, T. *I codici musicali contariniani del secolo XVII nella R. Biblioteca di S. Marco in Venezia.* (Venice) 1888.

WOLFF, H. *Die venezianische Oper in der zweiten Hälfte des 17. Jahrhunderts.* (Berlin) 1937.

WOTQUENNE, A. *Catalogue de la Bibliothèque du Conservatoire Royal de Musique de Bruxelles.* Annexe I. Libretti d'Opéras et d'Oratorios italiens du XVIIᵉ siècle. (Brussels) 1901.

ZUCKER, P. *Die Theaterdekoration des Barok.* (Berlin) 1925.

PUBLISHED SCORES OF OPERAS AND EXTRACTS FROM OPERAS PRODUCED IN VENICE 1637–1700

CAVALLI, F. *Venti arie tratte dai drami musicali di Francesco Cavalli.* (Vienna–Trieste) 1909.

—— 'Il Giasone', parts in *Gesellschaft für Musikforschung*, vol. xii, ed. Eitner (1883).

CESTI, A. 'La Dori', parts in *Gesellschaft für Musikforschung*, vol. xii, ed Eitner (1883).

DAVIDSON, A., and APEL, W., ed. *Historical Anthology of Music.* vol. 2. (London) 1950.

MANTICA, F., ed. *Prime fioriture del melodramma italiano*, 2 vols. (Rome) 1912–30.

MONTEVERDI, C. 'Il Ritorno d'Ulisse in patria', DTOe, vol. 29 (1).

—— —— ed. Malipiero, *Opere*, vol. xii.

—— 'L'incoronatione di Poppea', *Studien zur Geschichte der italienischen Oper im 17. Jahrhundert*, vol. ii, ed. Goldschmidt (1914).

—— —— 'Le Couronnement de Poppée', parts ed. d'Indy (1922).

—— —— Facsimile edition of the Venice score, ed. Benvenuti (1930).

—— —— ed. Malipiero, *Opere*, vol. xiii.

ROLLAND, R. 'Les Maîtres de l'opéra: recueil de musique inédite du XVIIᵉ et du XVIIIᵉ siècle', RHCM iii (1903).

MS. SOURCES

VENICE

Archivio di Stato. Busta 914. *Teatri Varii.*

Marciana. *Codici Contariniani.* 112 scores of operas produced in Venice during the seventeenth century.

Storia delle leggi e de' Costumi de' Veneziani (notebook of Giovanni Rossi).

Il Ritorno d'Ulisse in patria (libretto by Badovero).

LONDON

British Museum. Add. 14238. *Ercole in Tebe* (G. A. Boretti, 1670). Apart from an additional finale and some minor alterations this score agrees with that in the Marciana. Add. 29248. *La Dori* (Cesti).

Public Record Office. State Papers, Venice, 99/47, fos. 147–55. 99/48, fos. 168, 229. Details of Venetian life from notes by the English Resident, 1670.

Soane Museum. *Teatro di Tor di Nona del C. Carlo Fontana, di Roma, Firenze, Sienna, Fano.* This MS. contains a plan of SS. Giovanni e Paolo, Venice.

OXFORD

Bodleian Library. Rawlinson MS. C 799, fos. 162–3 and 173–4. Robert Bargrave describes the opera and singing in Venice, 1655.

PARIS

Bibliothèque Nationale. Rés. V 2566. Ballet from *La Finta Pazza* (Balbi). Yf 850. Ballet from *Xerxes* (Cavalli).

Bibliothèque de l'Opéra. Rés. C 670. *Dissegni dell' opere rappresentate nel treatro di S. Salvatore di Venetia, l'anno 1675.*

VIENNA

National Library. MS. 18763. *Il Ritorno d'Ulisse in patria* (Monteverdi).

Supplementary Bibliography (September 1968)

ABERT, A. A. *Claudio Monteverdi und das musikalische Drama.* (Lippstadt) 1954.

ARNOLD, D. 'Music at the Scuola di San Rocco', M & L xl (1959). 'Francesco Cavalli: Some recently discovered documents', M & L xlvi (1965). *Monteverdi.* (London) 1963.

BJURSTRÖM, P. *Giacomo Torelli and Baroque Stage Design.* (Stockholm) 1962.

CIVITA, A. *Ottavio Rinuccini e il sorgere del melodramma in Italia.* (Mantua) 1900.

DELLA CORTE, A. *Dramma per musica dal Rinuccini allo Zeno.* 2 vols. (Turin) [1958].

GHISLANZONI, A. *Luigi Rossi (Aloysius de Rubeis), biographia e analisi delle composizioni.* (Milan & Rome) [1954].

GROUT, D. J. 'The Chorus in Early Opera', *Festschrift Friedrich Blume.* (Kassel and Basle) 1963.

GUIET, R. 'L'Évolution d'un genre: le livret d'opéra en France de Gluck a la Révolution', *Smith College studies in Modern Languages.* vol. XVIII (1936-7).

HERIOT, A. *The Castrati in Opera.* (London) 1956.

LOEWENBERG, A. *Annals of opera, 1597-1940.* 2nd revised ed. (Geneva), 1955.

MAGAGNATO, L. *Teatri italiani del Cinquecento.* (Venice) 1954.

OSTHOFF, W. *Das dramatische Spätwerk Claudi Monteverdis.* (Tutzing) 1960.

PETROBELLI, P. 'L'Ermiona' di Pio Eneo degli Obizzi ed i primi spettacoli d'opera veneziani', *La Nuova Musicologia italiana.* Quaderna della Rass M vol. 3 (Turin) 1965.

ROBINSON, M. F. *Opera before Mozart.* (London) 1966.

ROSE, G. 'Agazzari and the Improving Orchestra', *Journal of the American Musicological Society.* XVII (1964).

ROSENTHAL, A. 'A hitherto unpublished letter of Claudio Monteverdi', *Essays presented to Egon Wellesz.* (Oxford) 1966.

SCHILD, M. *Die Musikdramen Ottavio Rinuccinis.* (Munich) 1933.

SCHRADE, L. *La Représentation d'Edipo Tiranno au Teatro Olimpico.* (Paris) 1960.

SOLERTI, A. *Gli albori del melodramma.* 3 vols. (Milan) 1904.

STEVENS, D., and FORTUNE, N. (eds.) *The Monteverdi Companion.* (London) 1968.

STRONG, R. *Festival Designs by Inigo Jones.* International Exhibition Foundation (1967-8).

TOWNELEY, S. 'Metastasio as a librettist', *Art and Ideas in eighteenth-century Italy.* (Rome) 1960.

WEAVER, R. L. 'Orchestra in Early Italian Opera', *Journal of the American Musicological Society.* XVII (1964).

WOLFF, H. C. *Die Barockoper in Hamburg.* (Wolfenbüttel) 1957.

PUBLISHED SCORES
CAVALLI, F. *L'Ormindo*, fac. ed. (London) 1968.

MS. SOURCES
VENICE

Marciana. Caffi, Fr.
Storia della musica teatrale a Venezia. It. IV, 747-9.
Aggiunte alla storia della musica sacra a Venezia. It. IV, 762.

Index to the Musical Examples

General Index